PUG COLORING BOOK

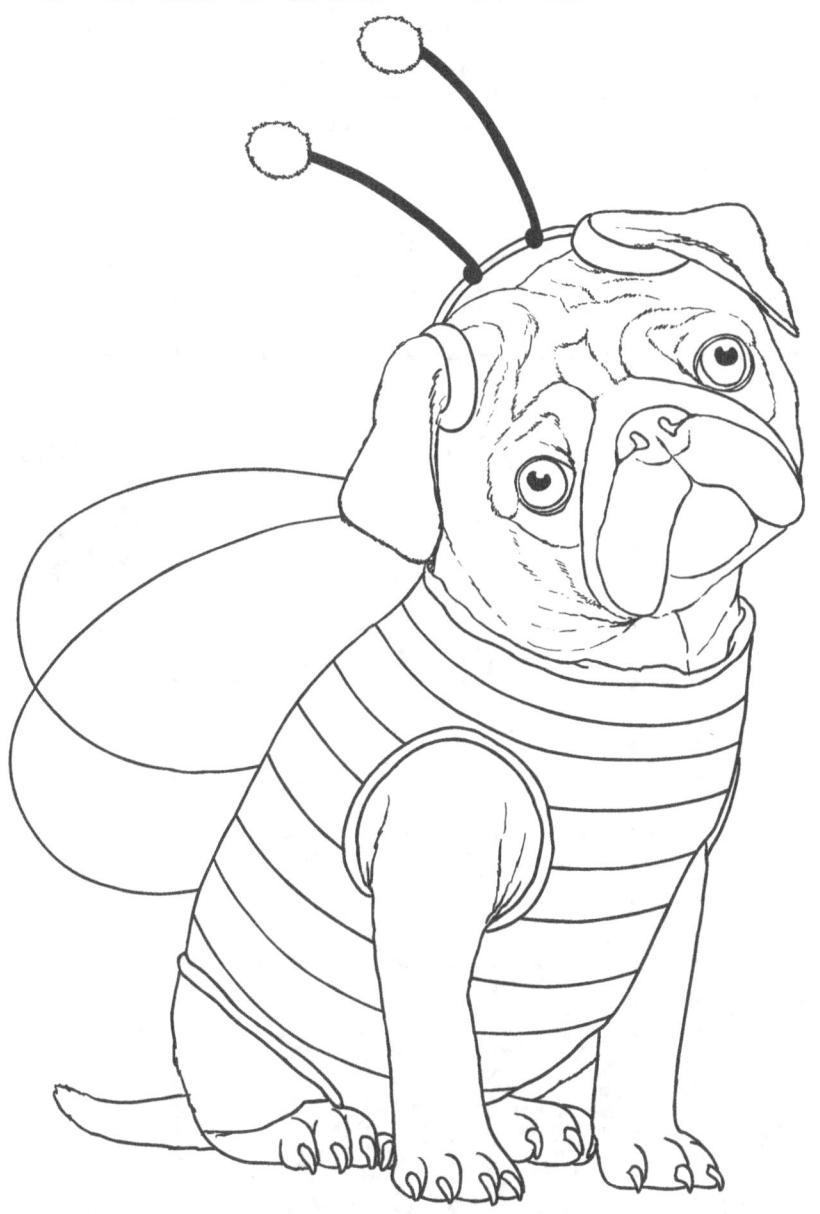

— RUSS FOCUS —

ISBN-13: 978-1727172560   ISBN-10: 1727172566
PUBLISHED BY RUSS FOCUS COPYRIGHT © 2018 ALL RIGHTS RESERVED
NO PART OF THIS PUBLICATION MAY BE REPRODUCED IN ANY
FORM OR BY ANY MEANS WITHOUT WRITTEN PERMISSION OF THE PUBLISHER.
WE ARE NOT RESPONSIBLE FOR UNSOLICITES MATERIAL PUBLISHED IN USA

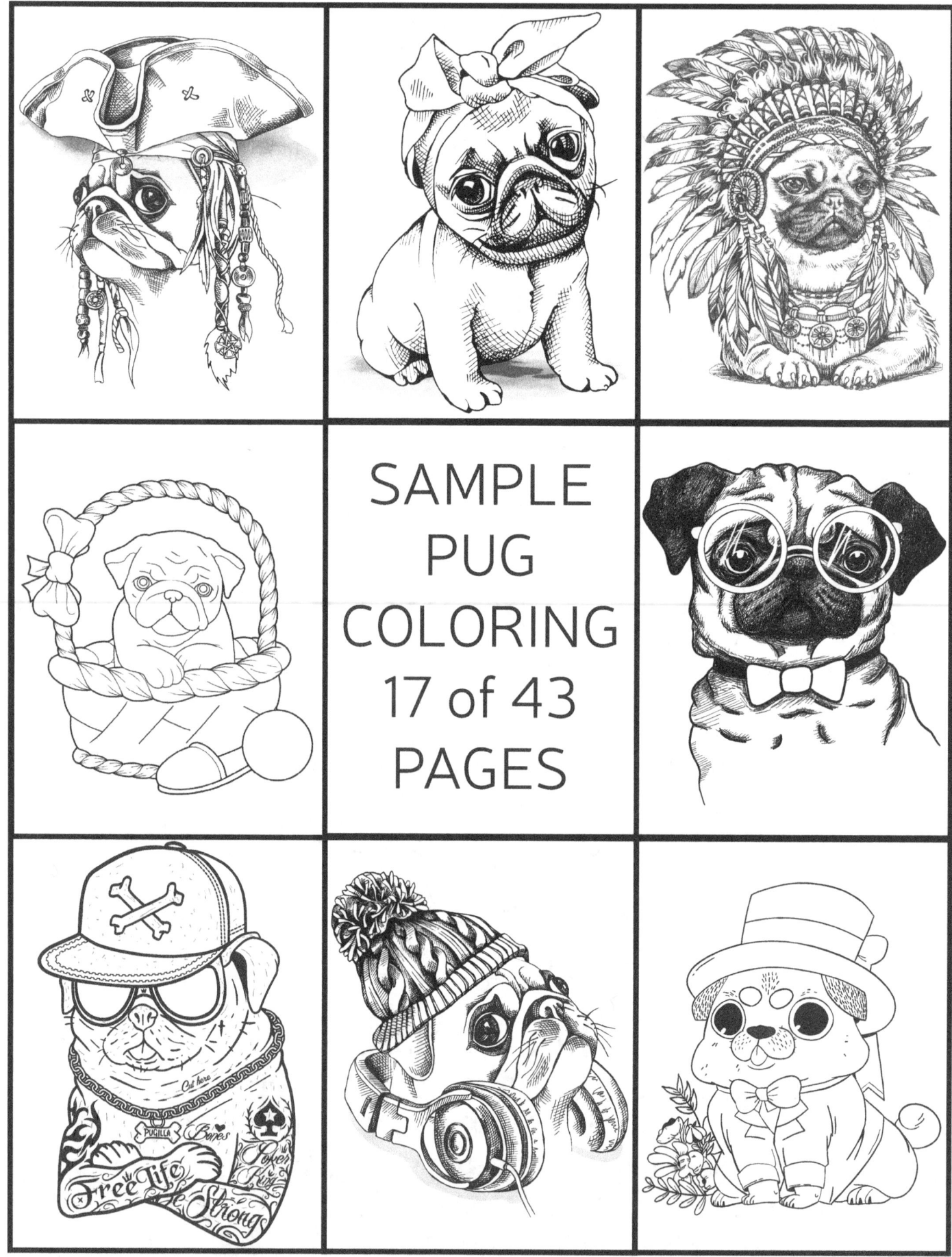

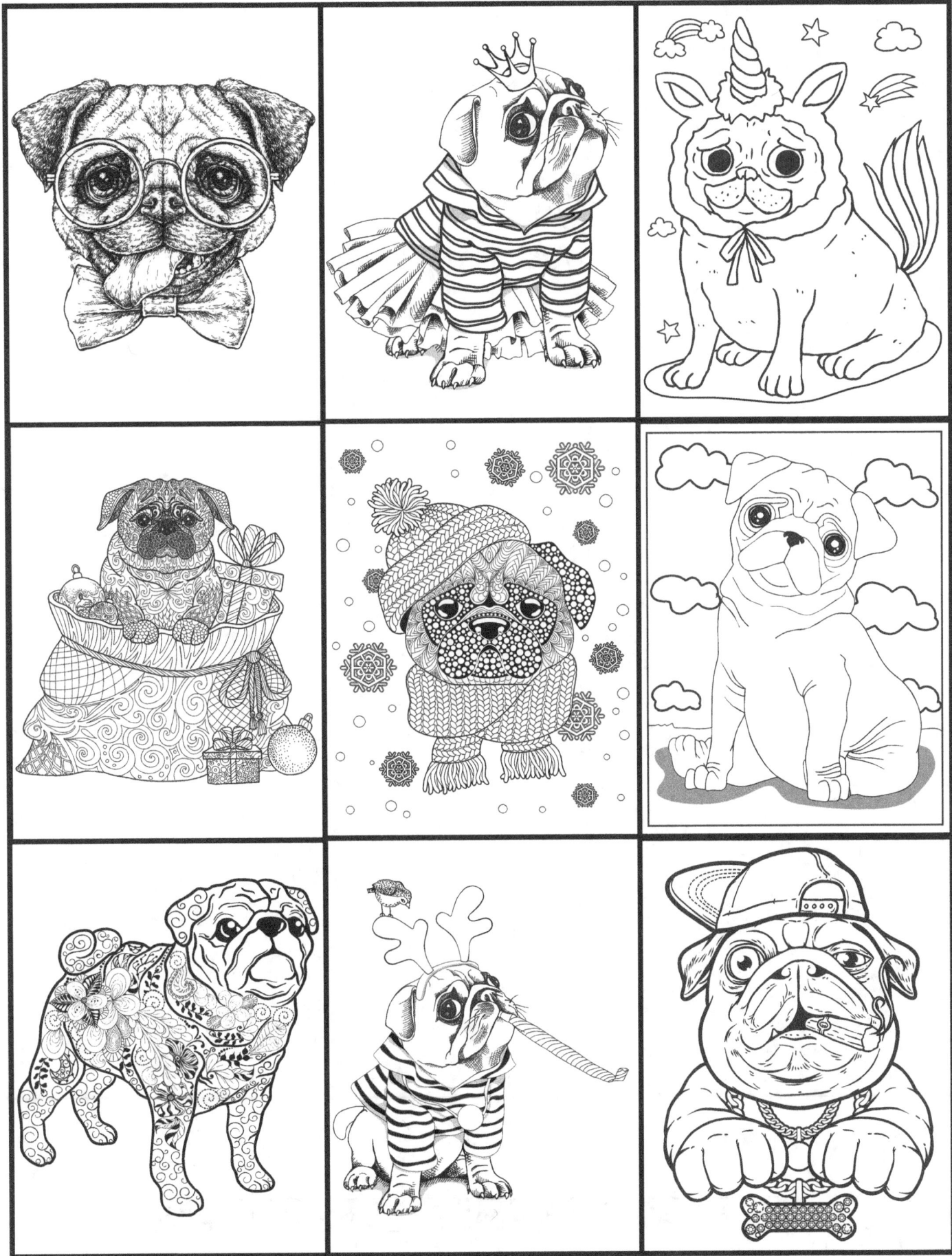

www.russfocus.com

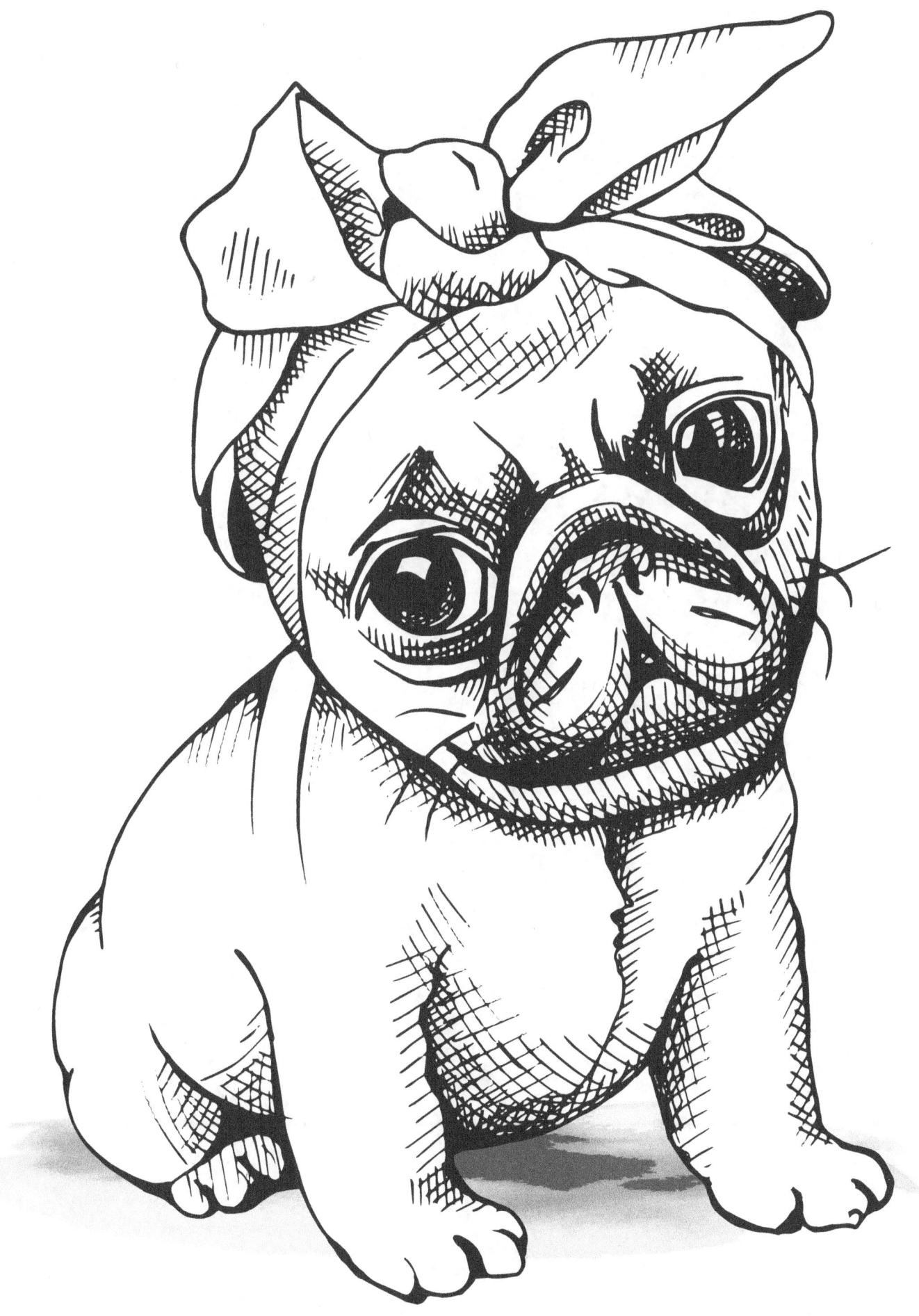

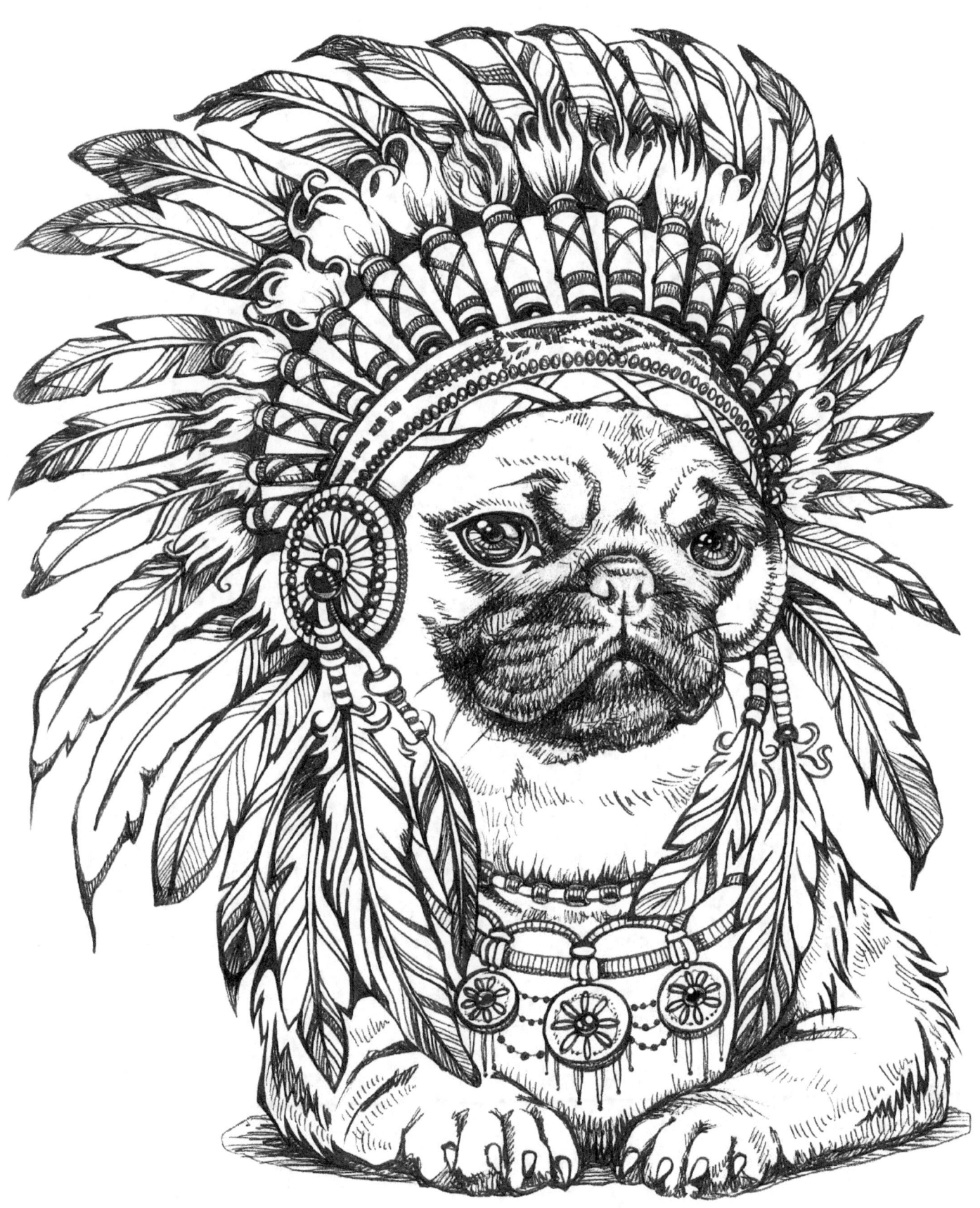

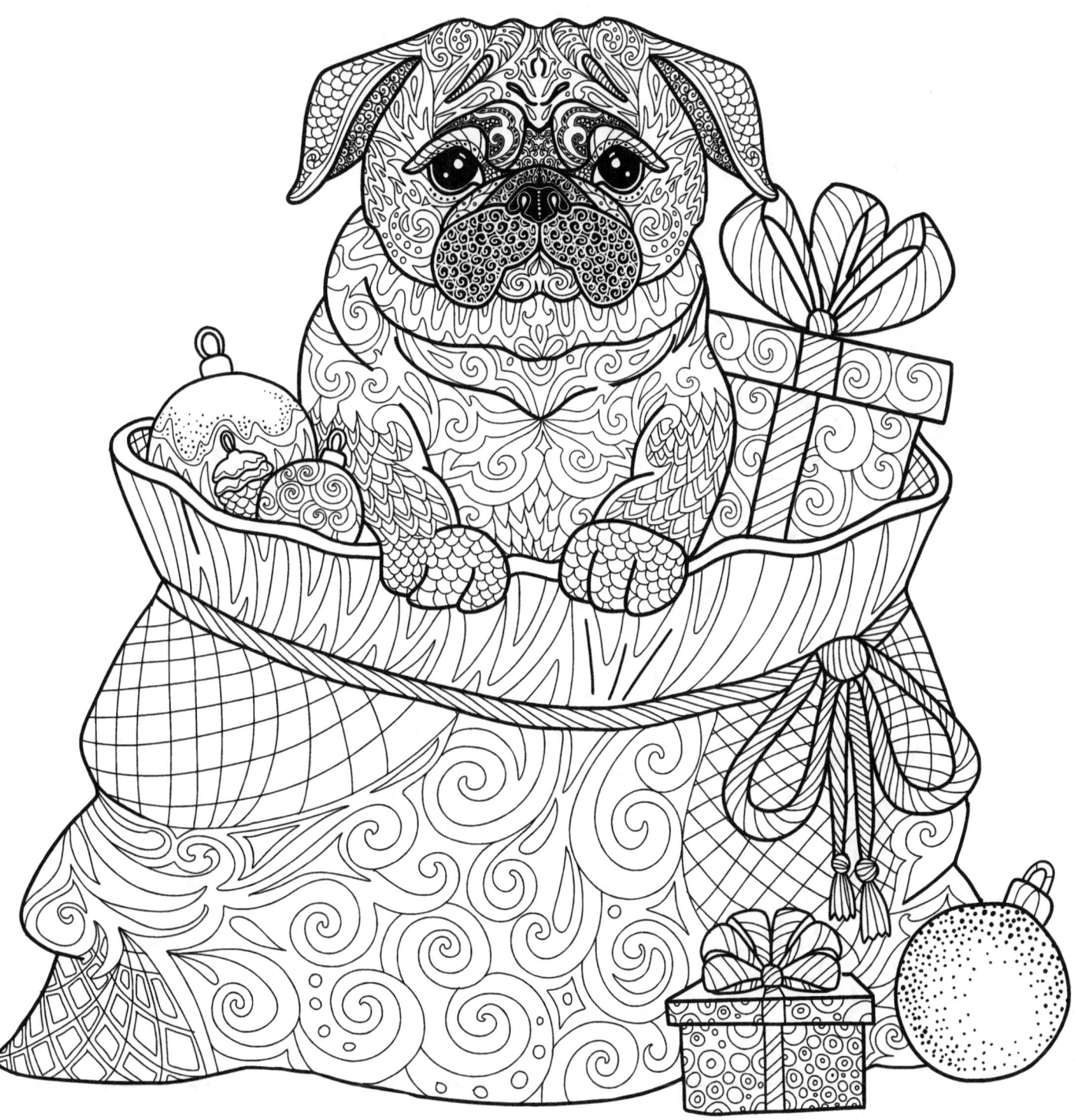

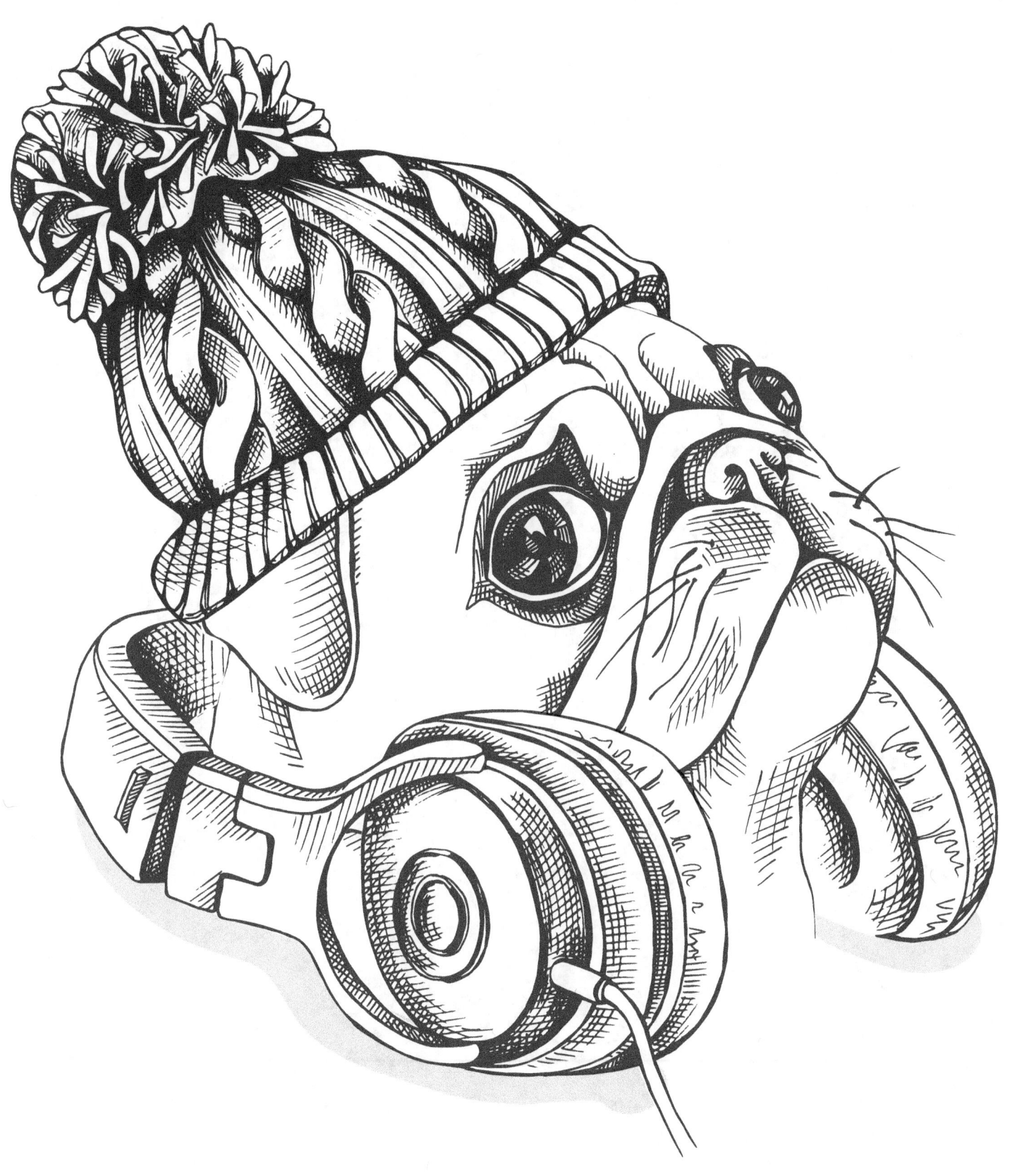

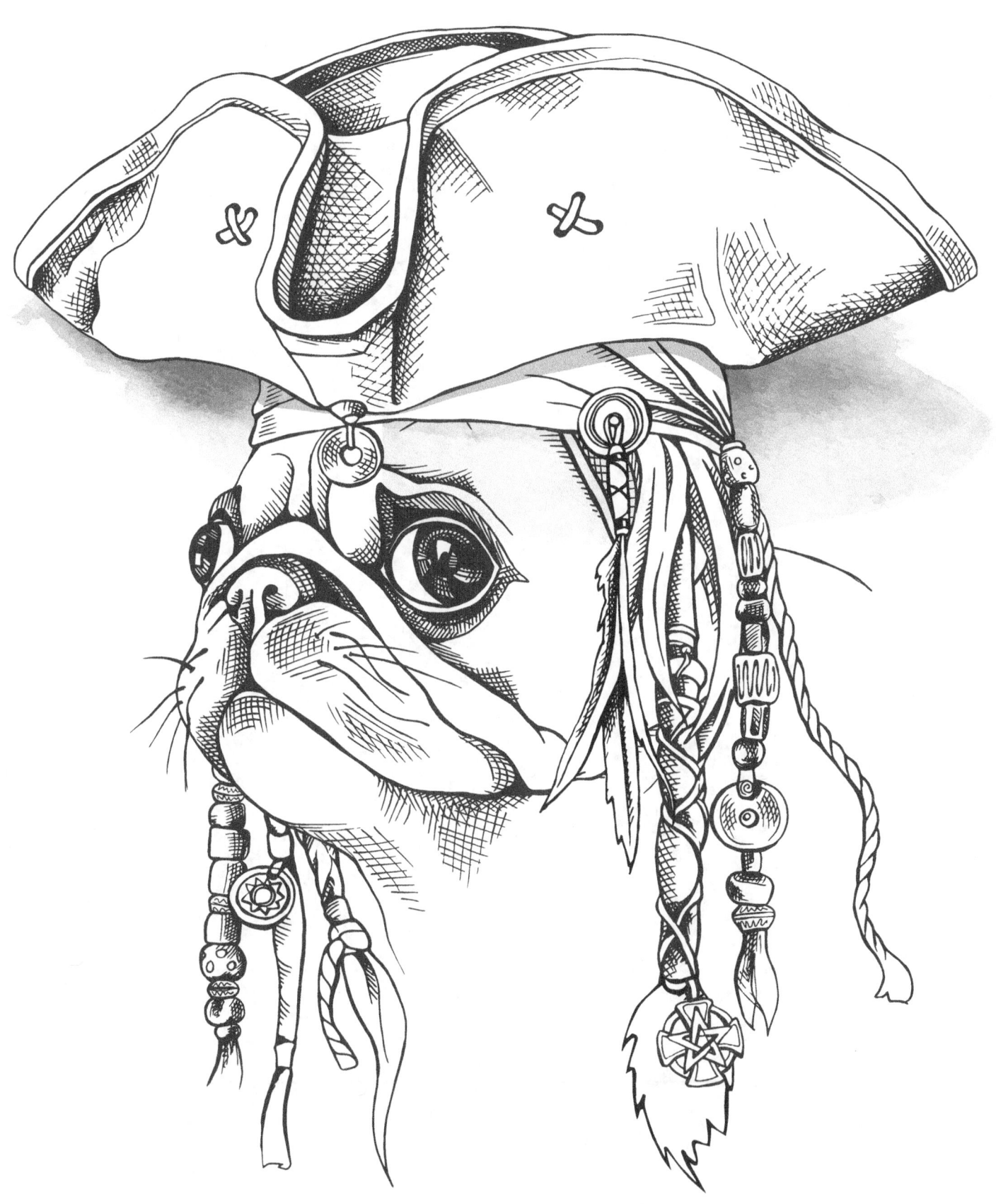

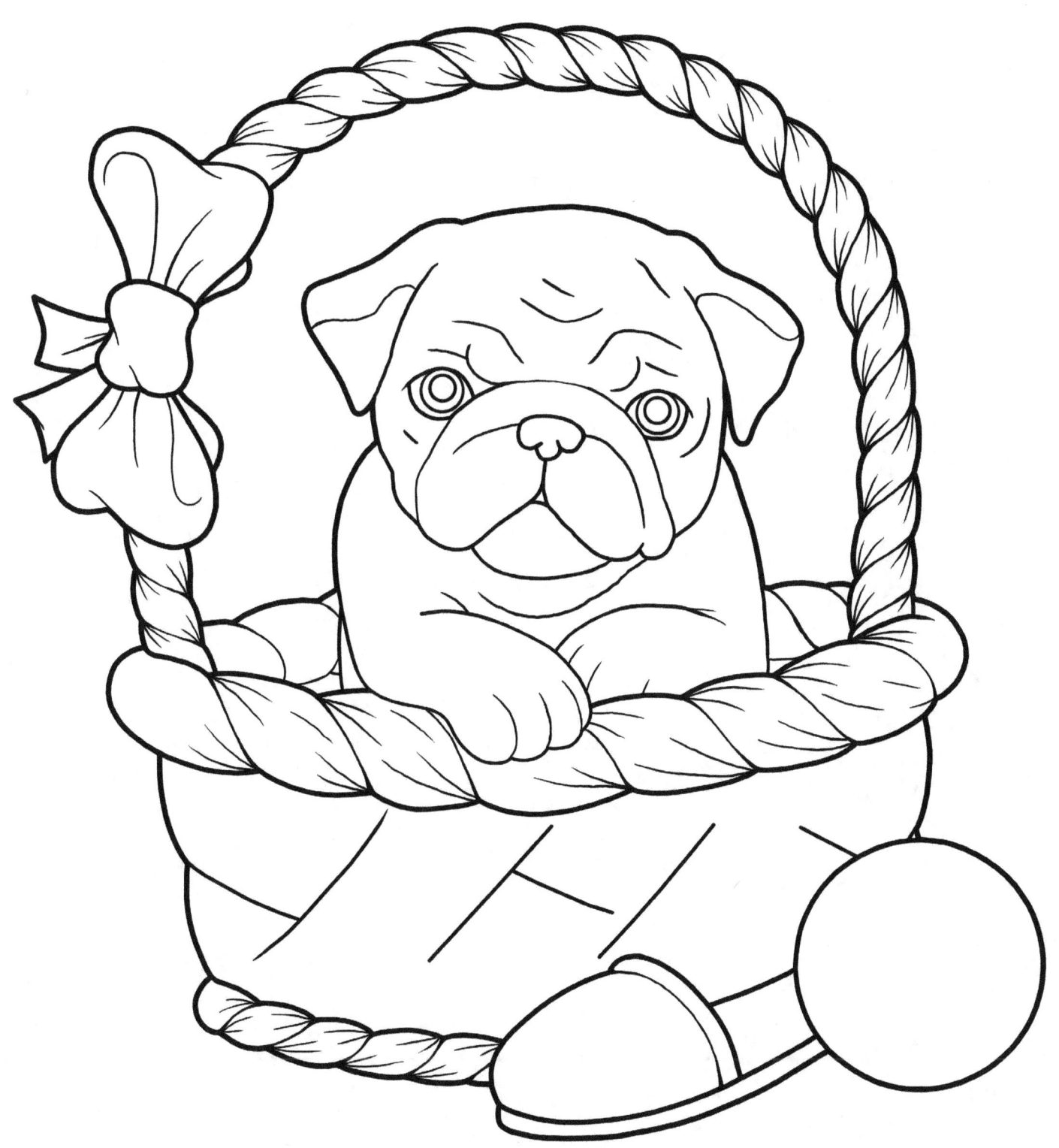

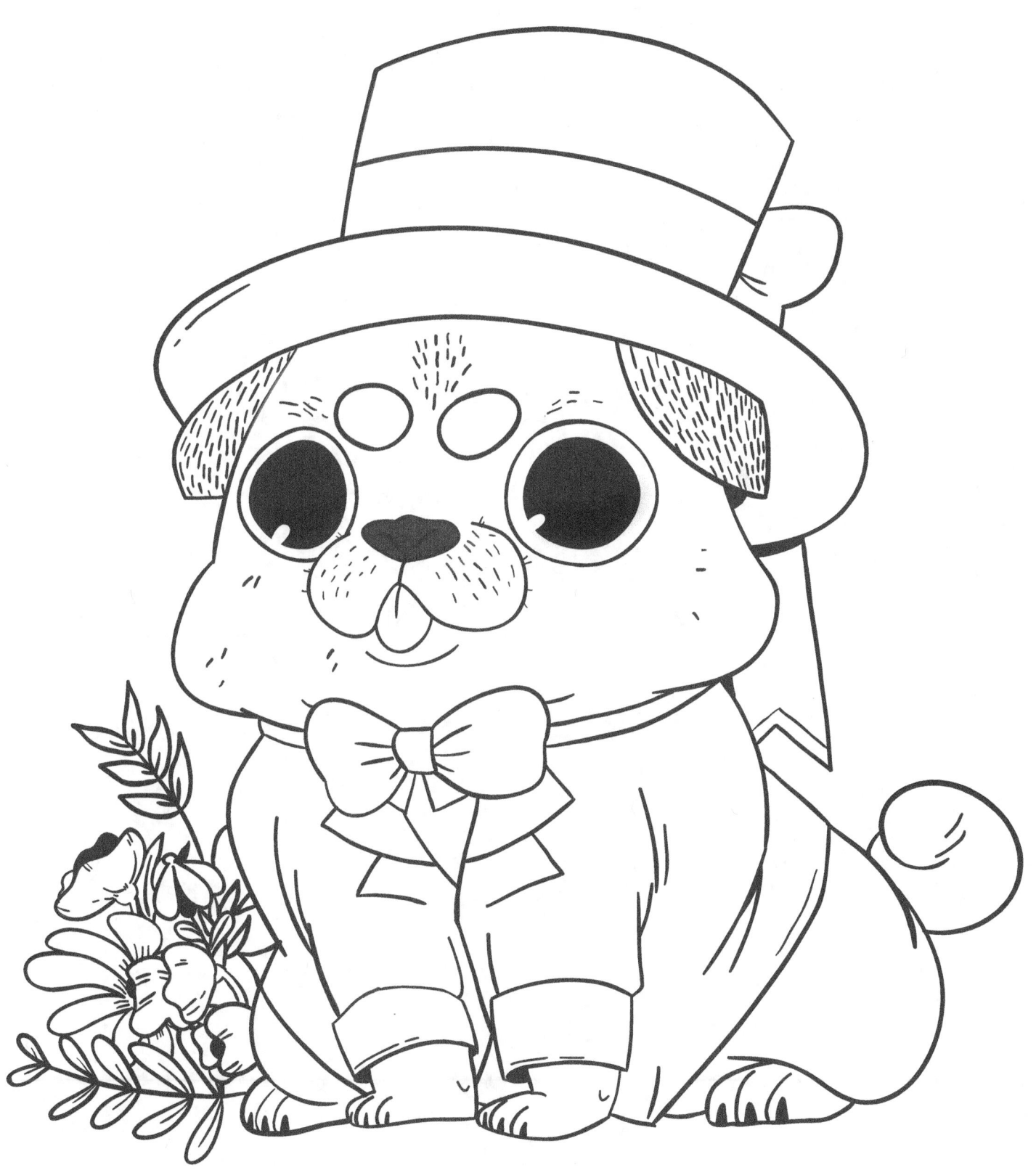

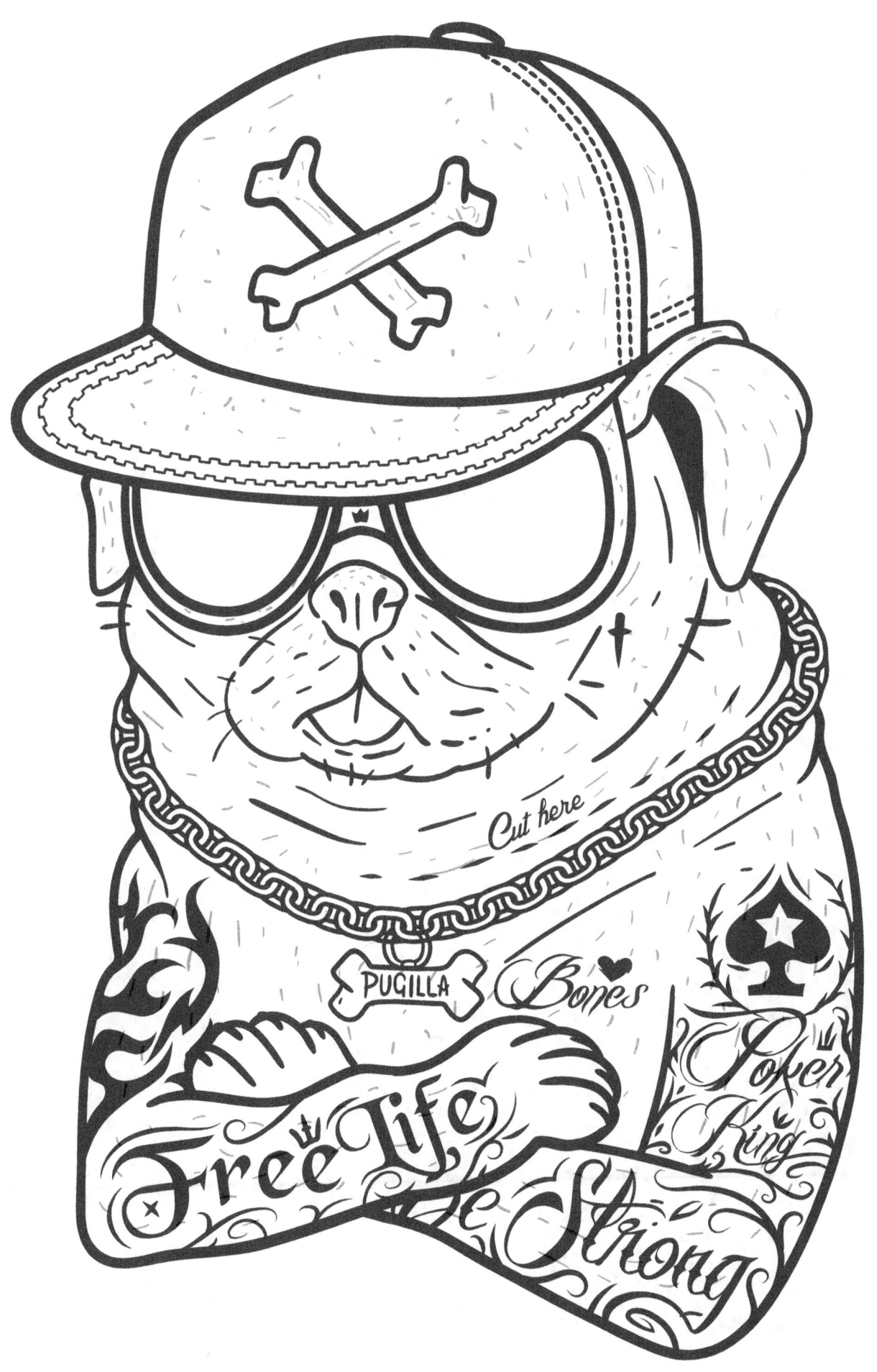

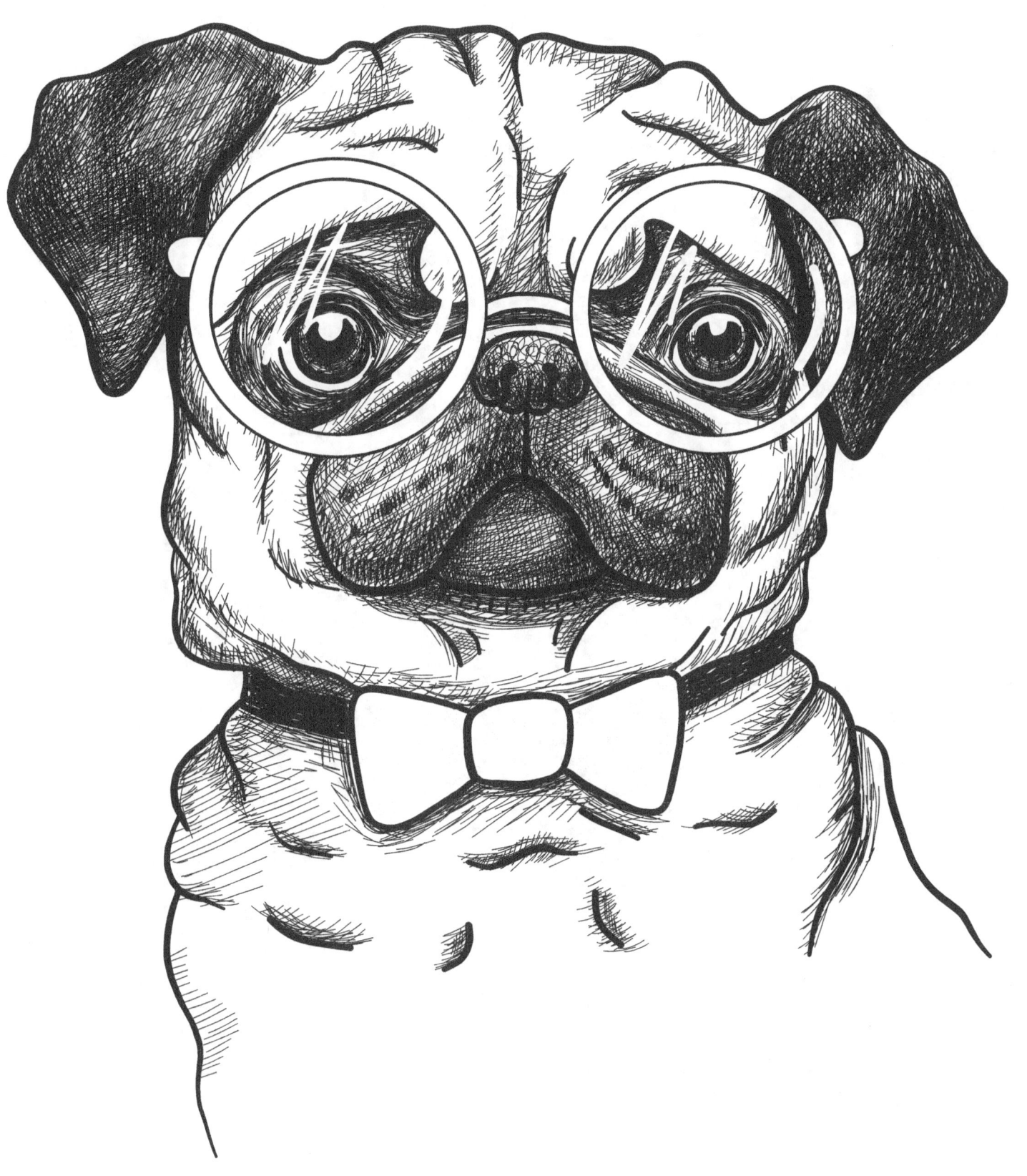

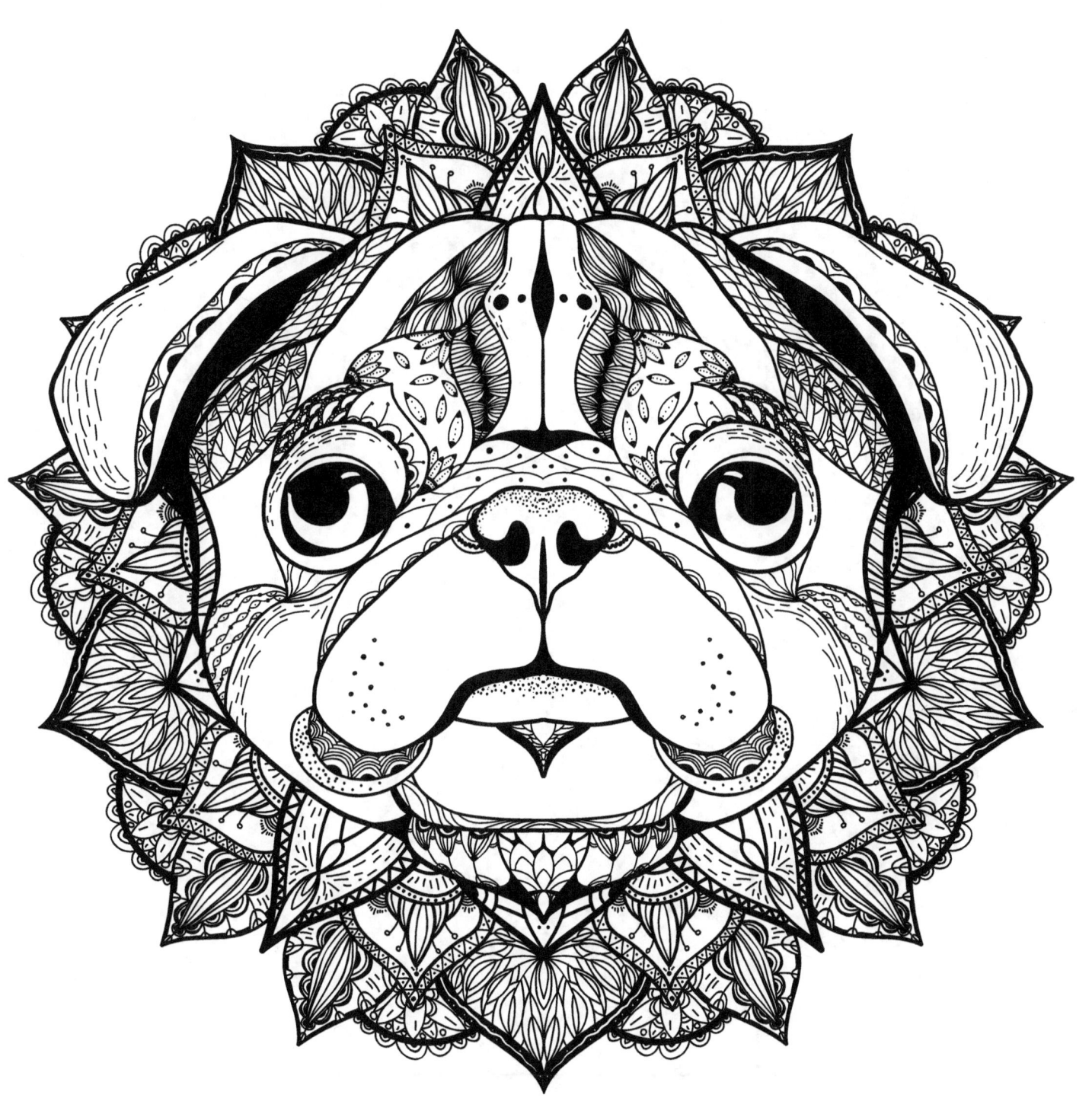

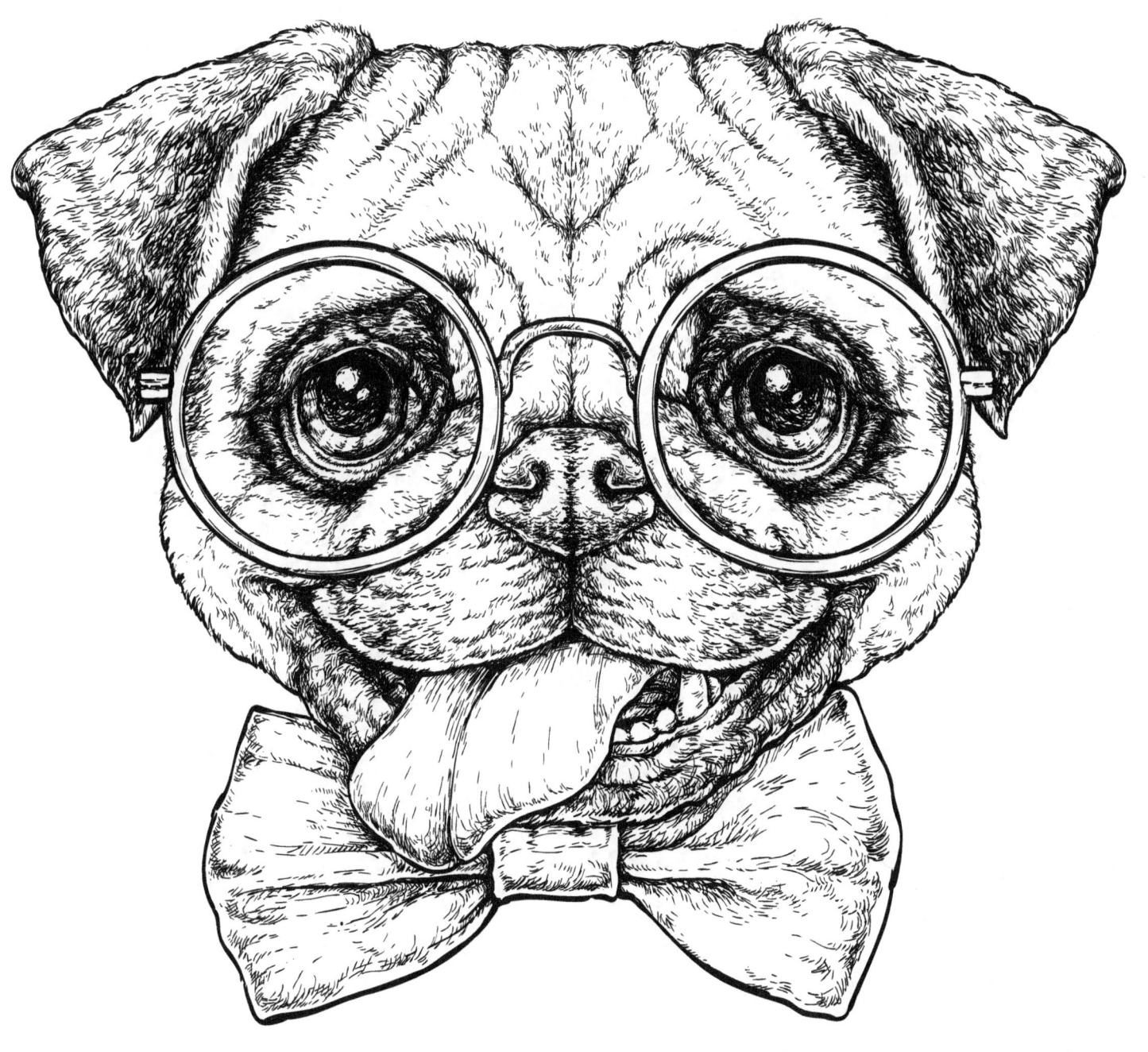

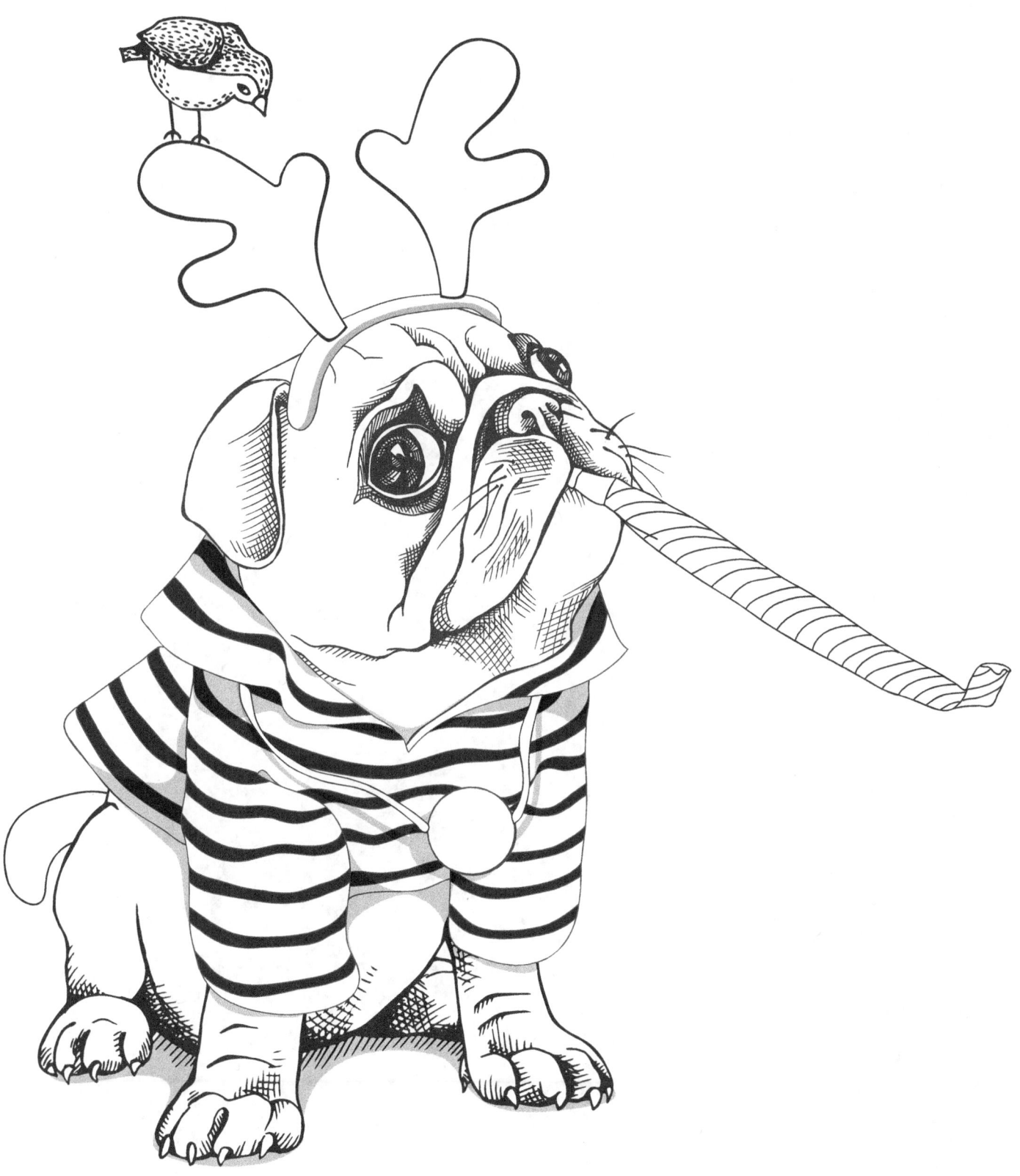

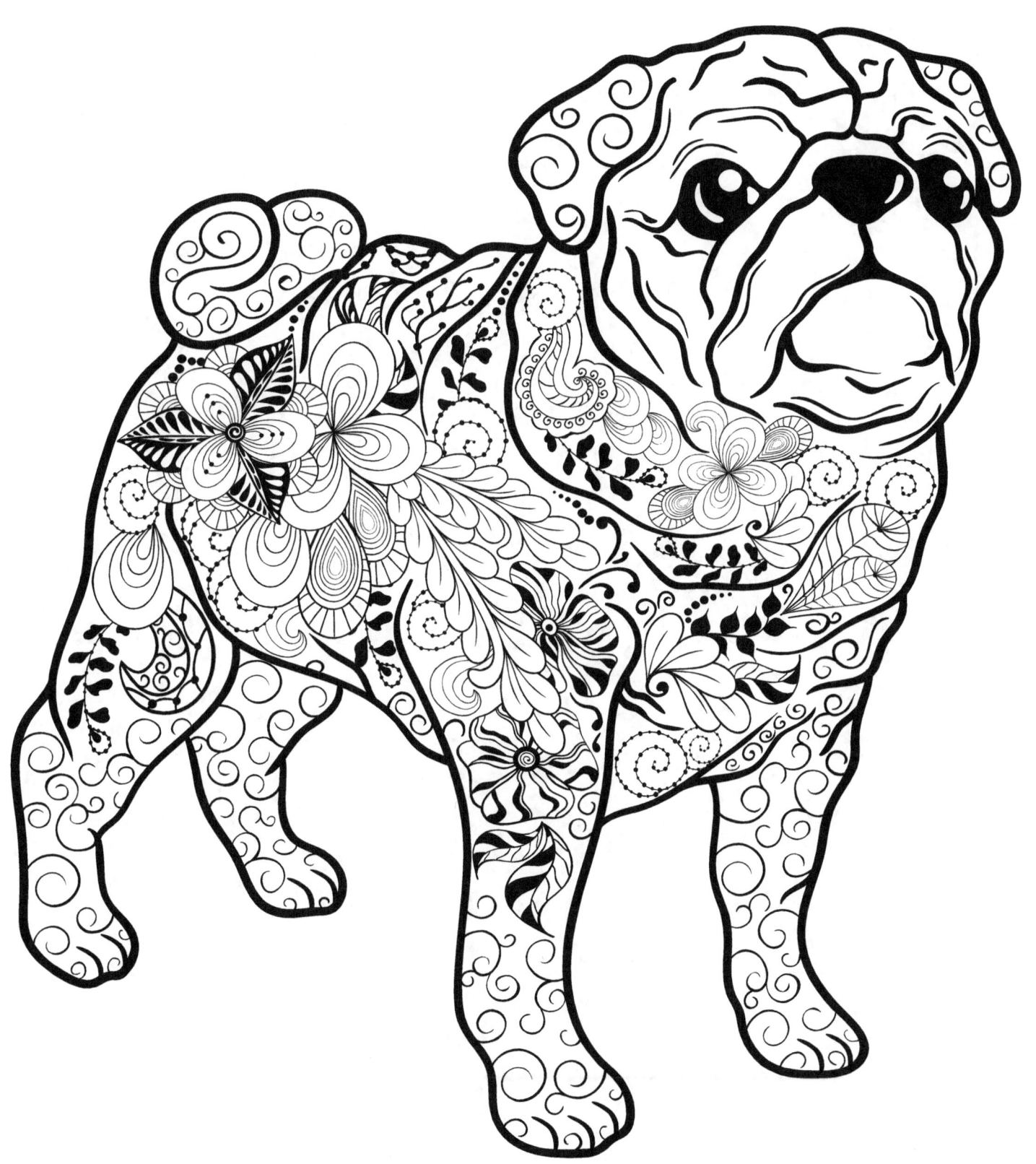

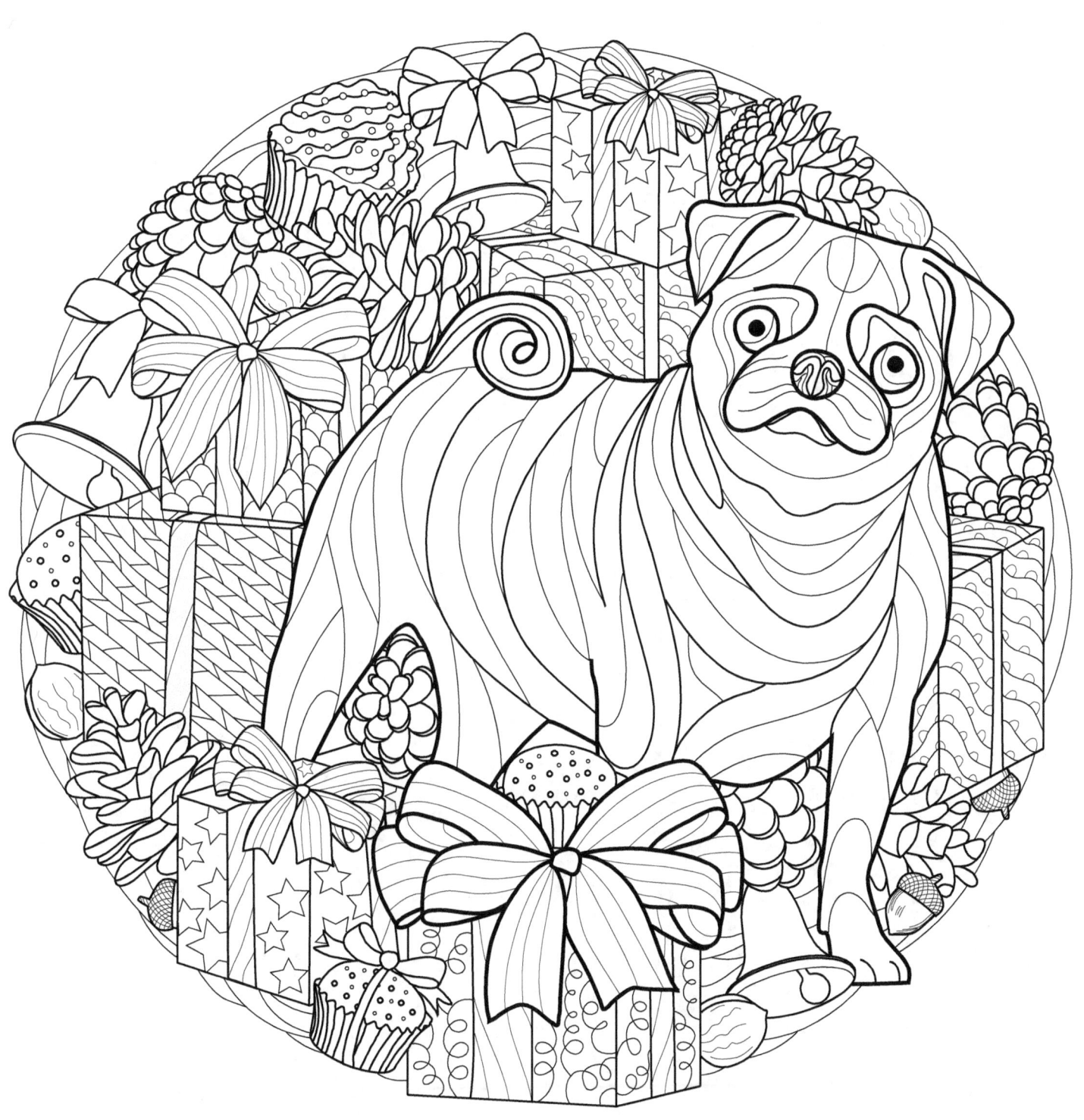

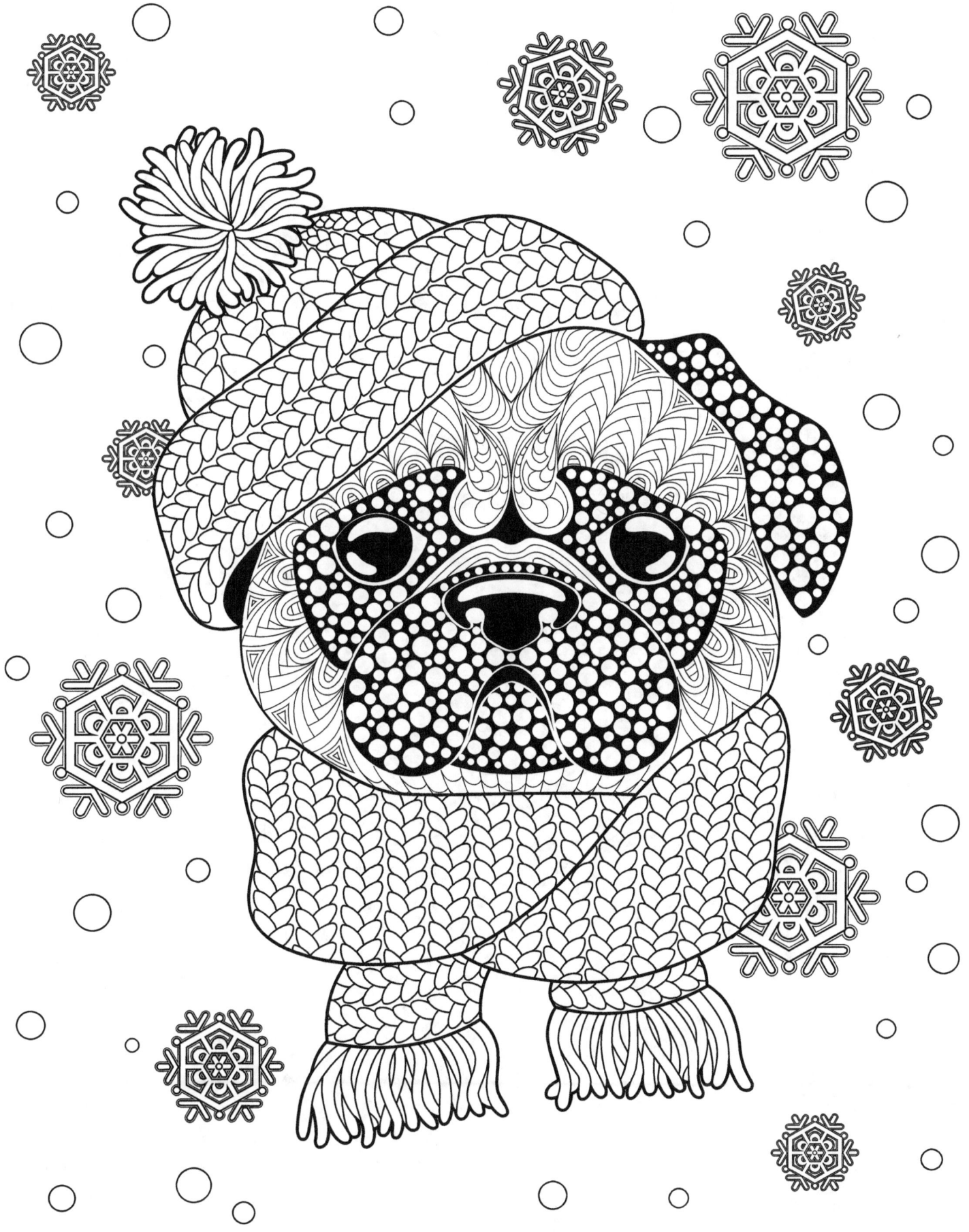

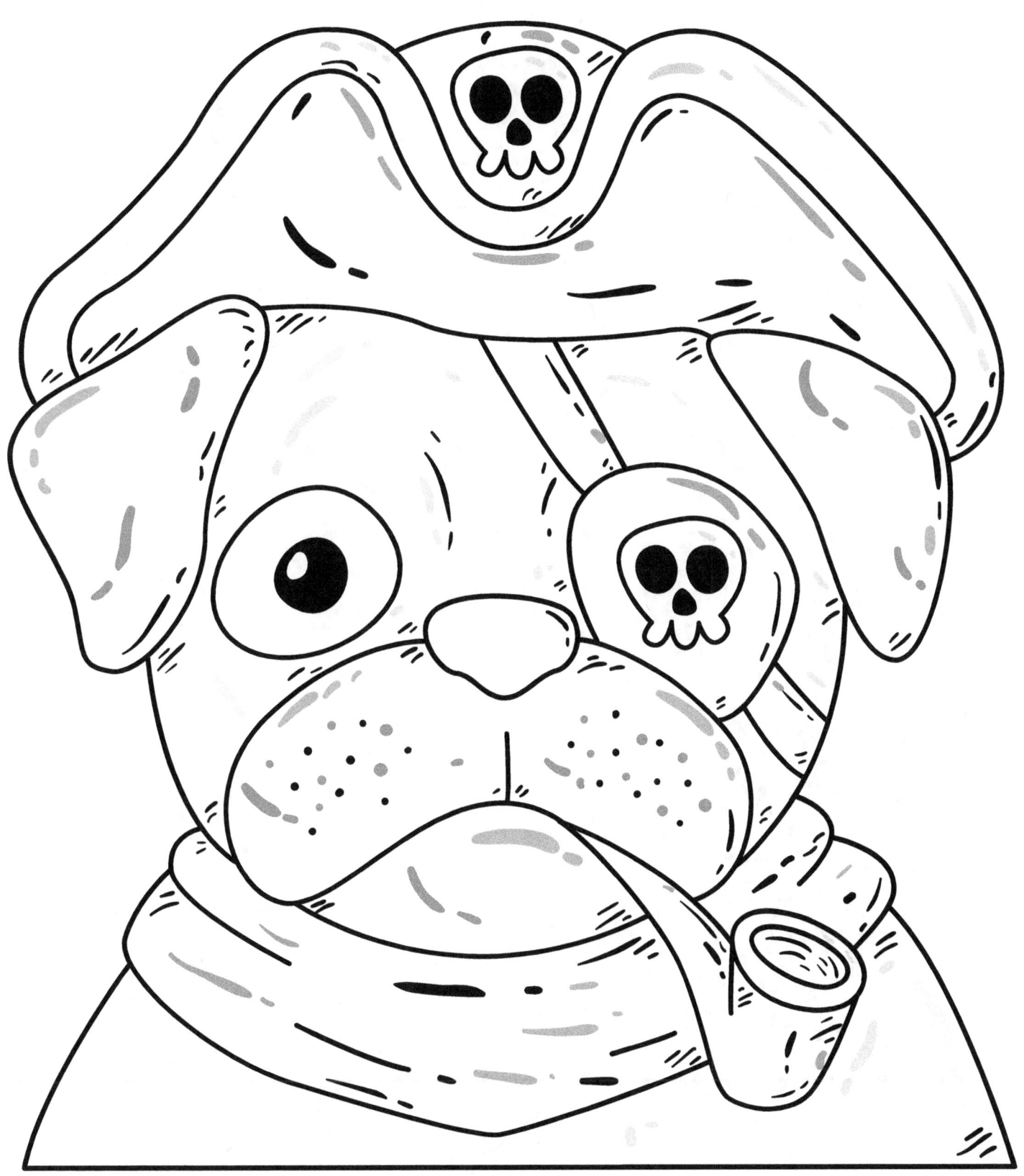

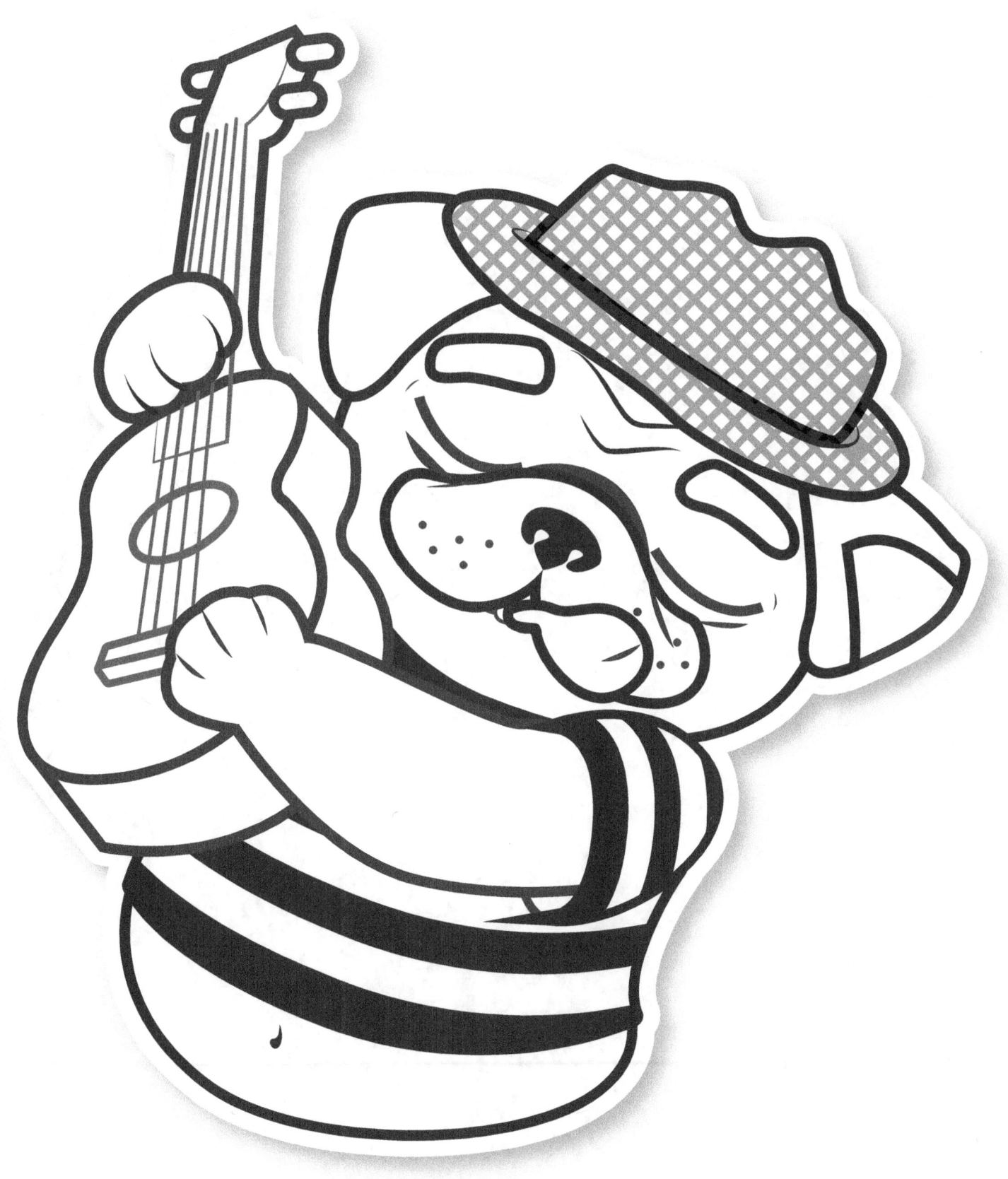

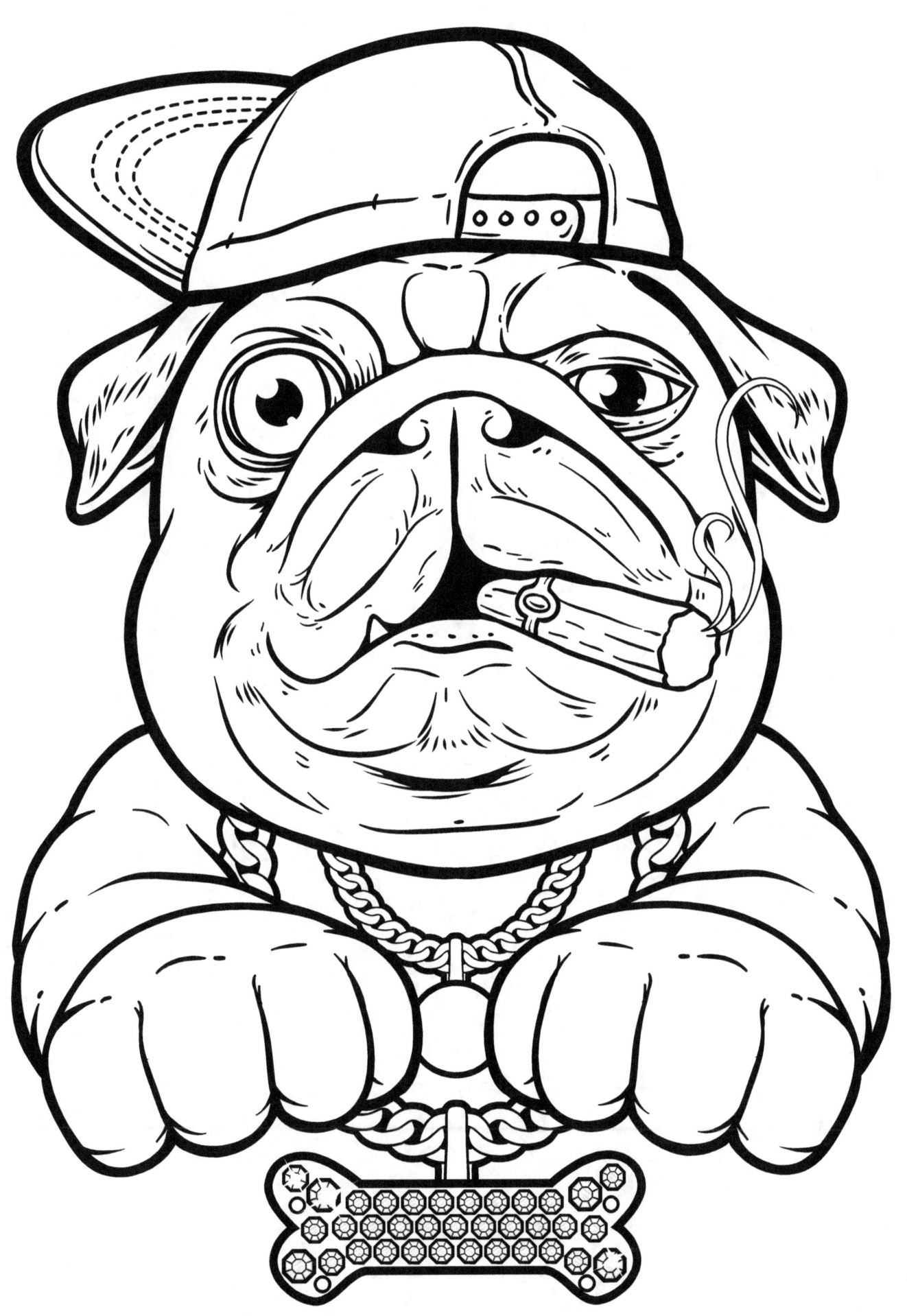

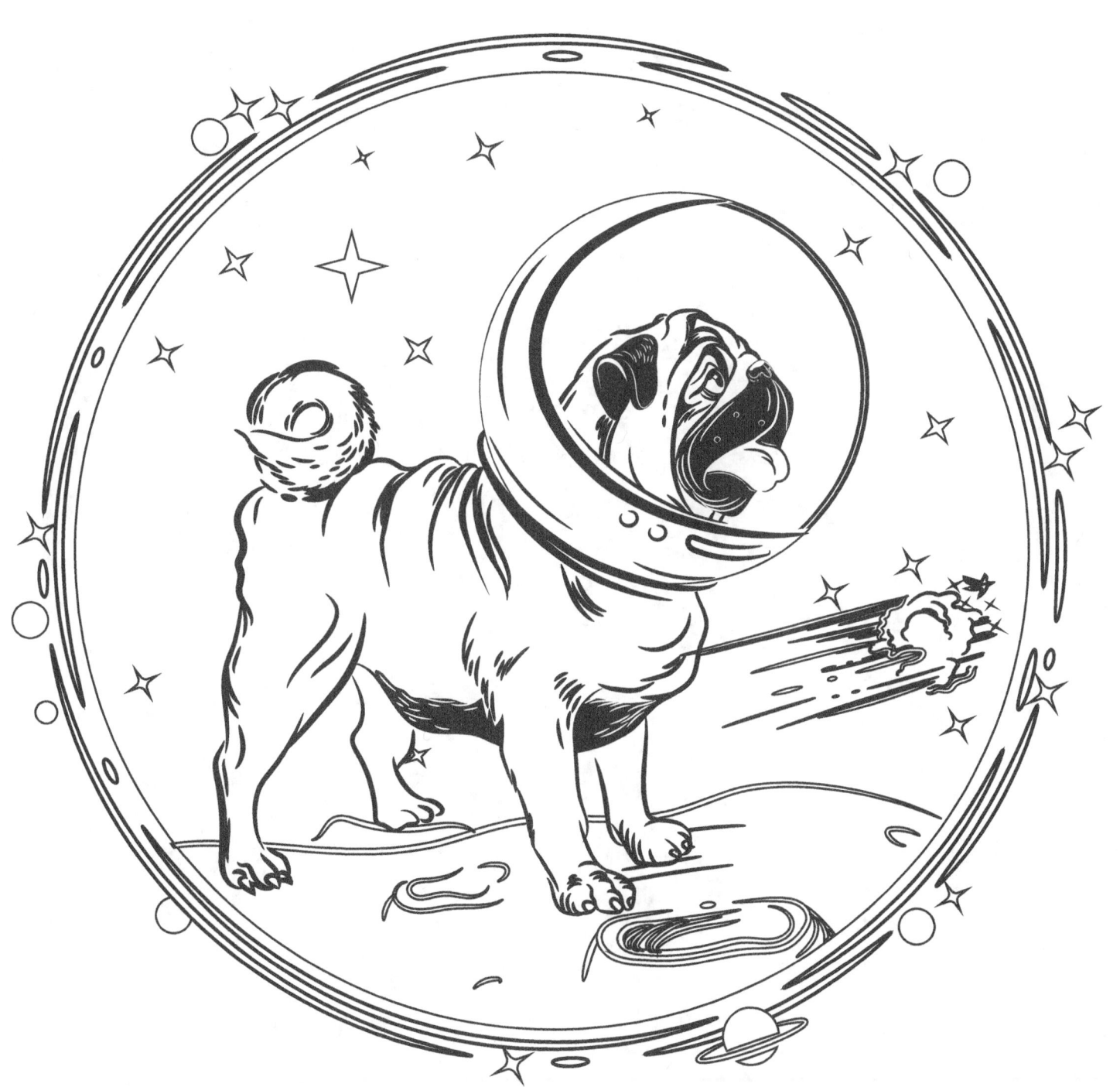

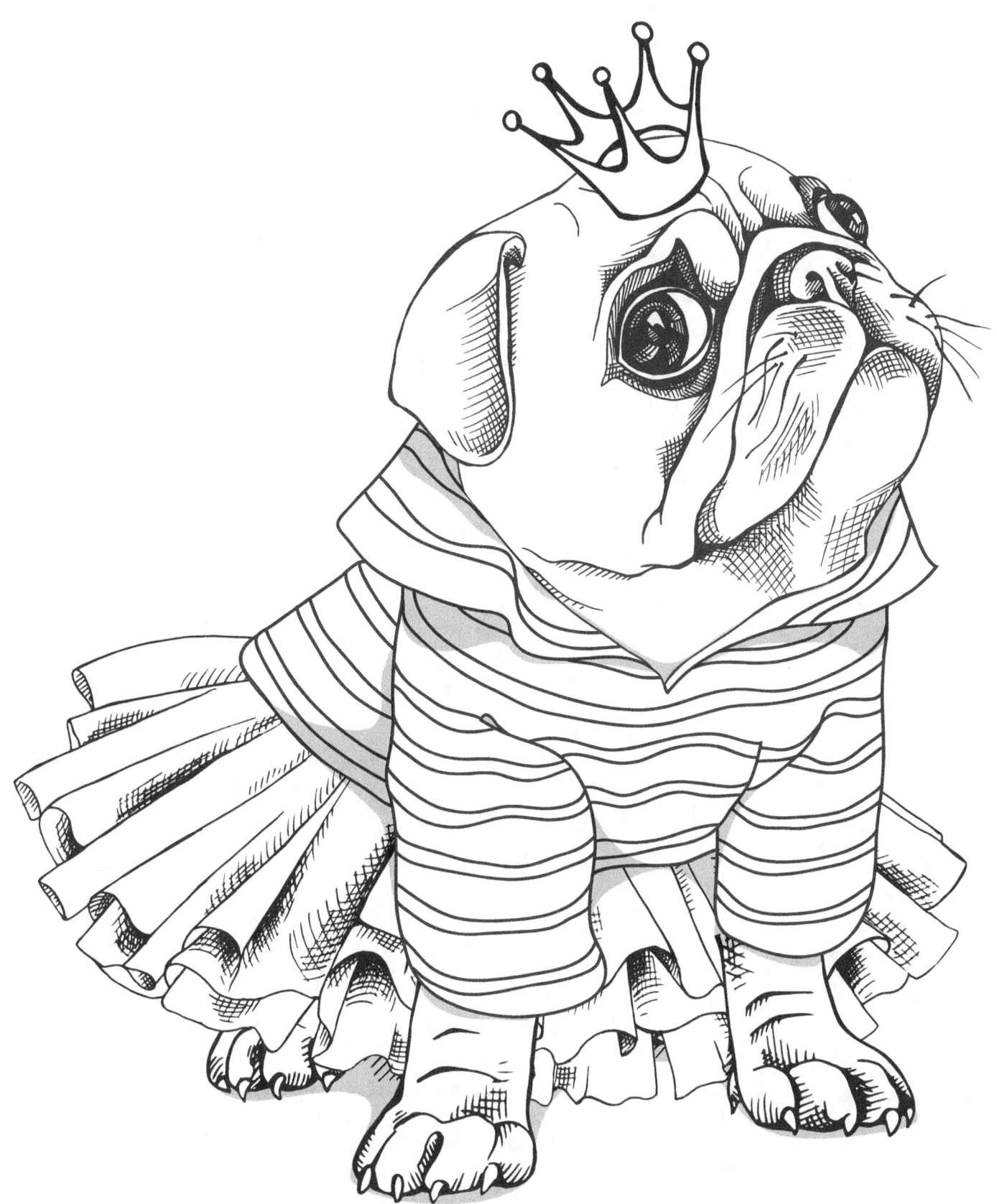

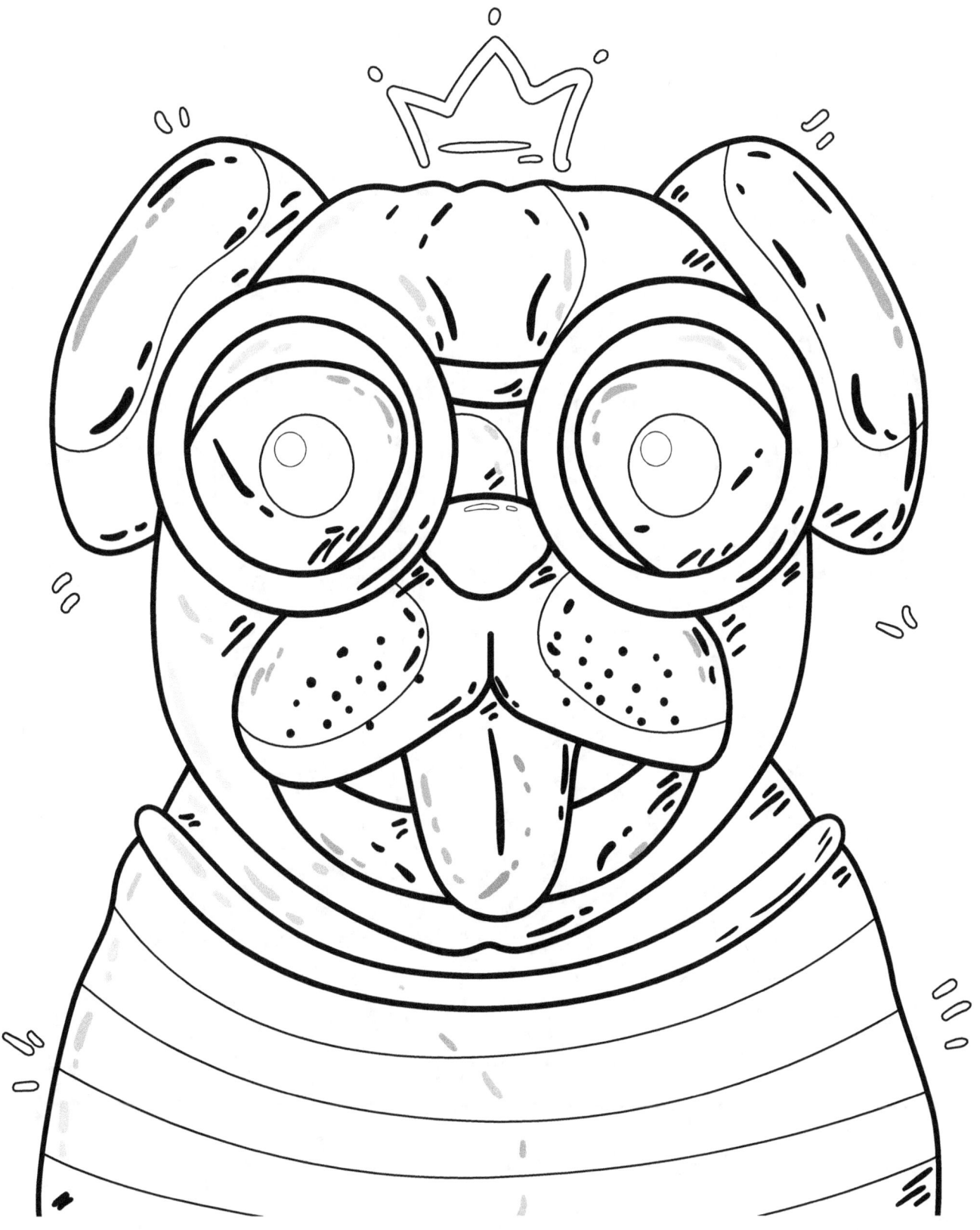

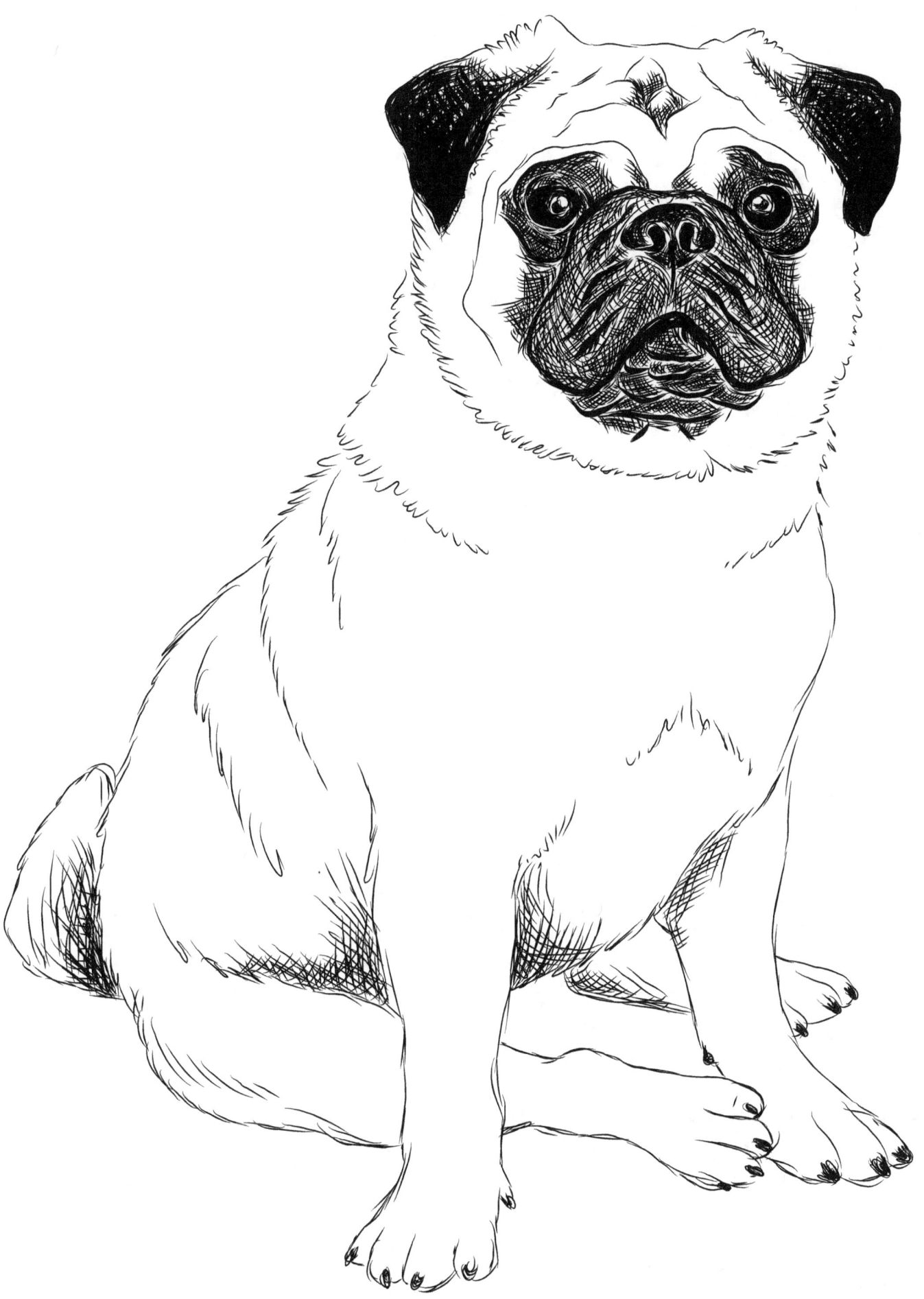

2'0"

1'5"

1'0"

9781569978014

BAD PUGGY

charge : you don't wanna know!

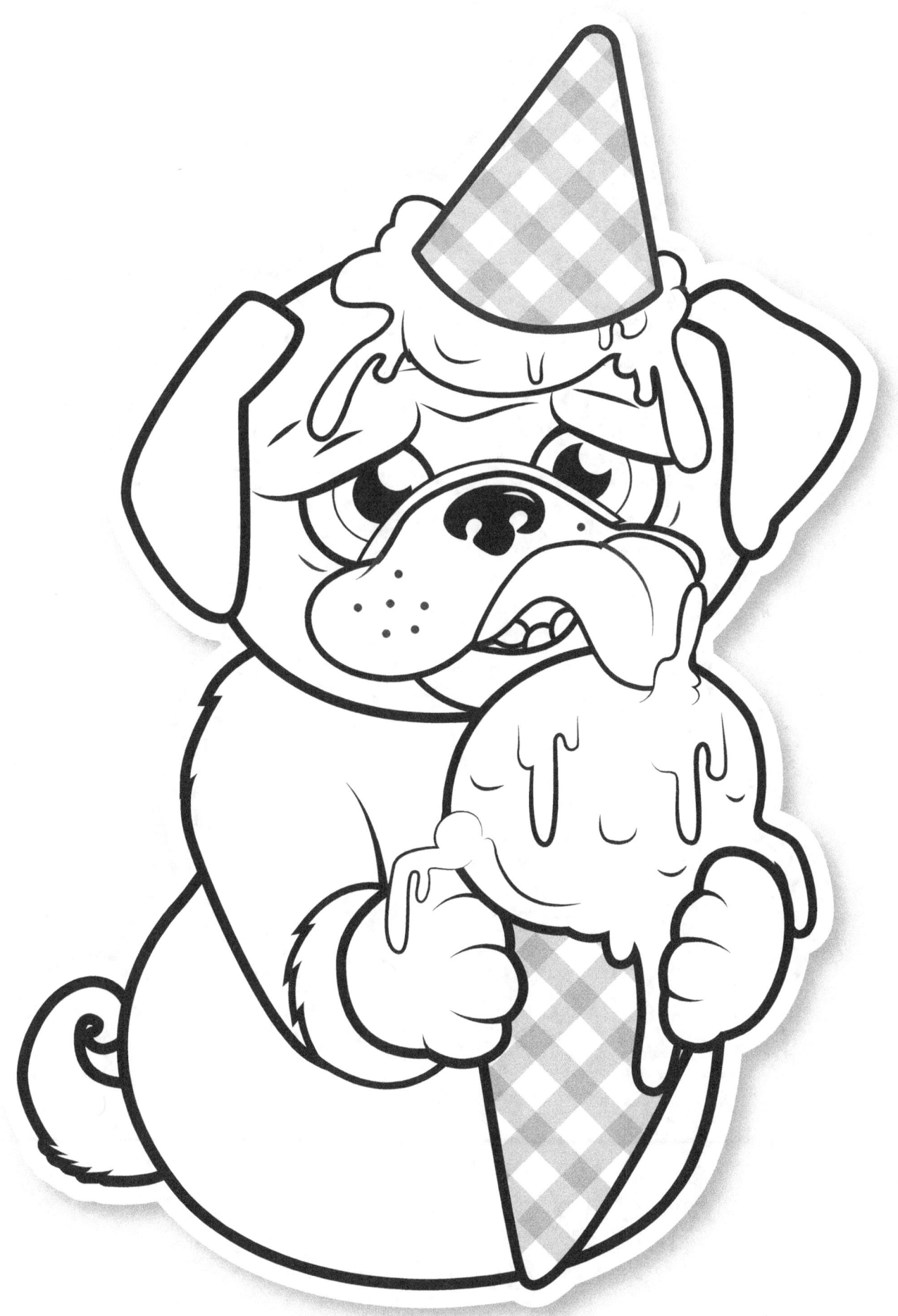

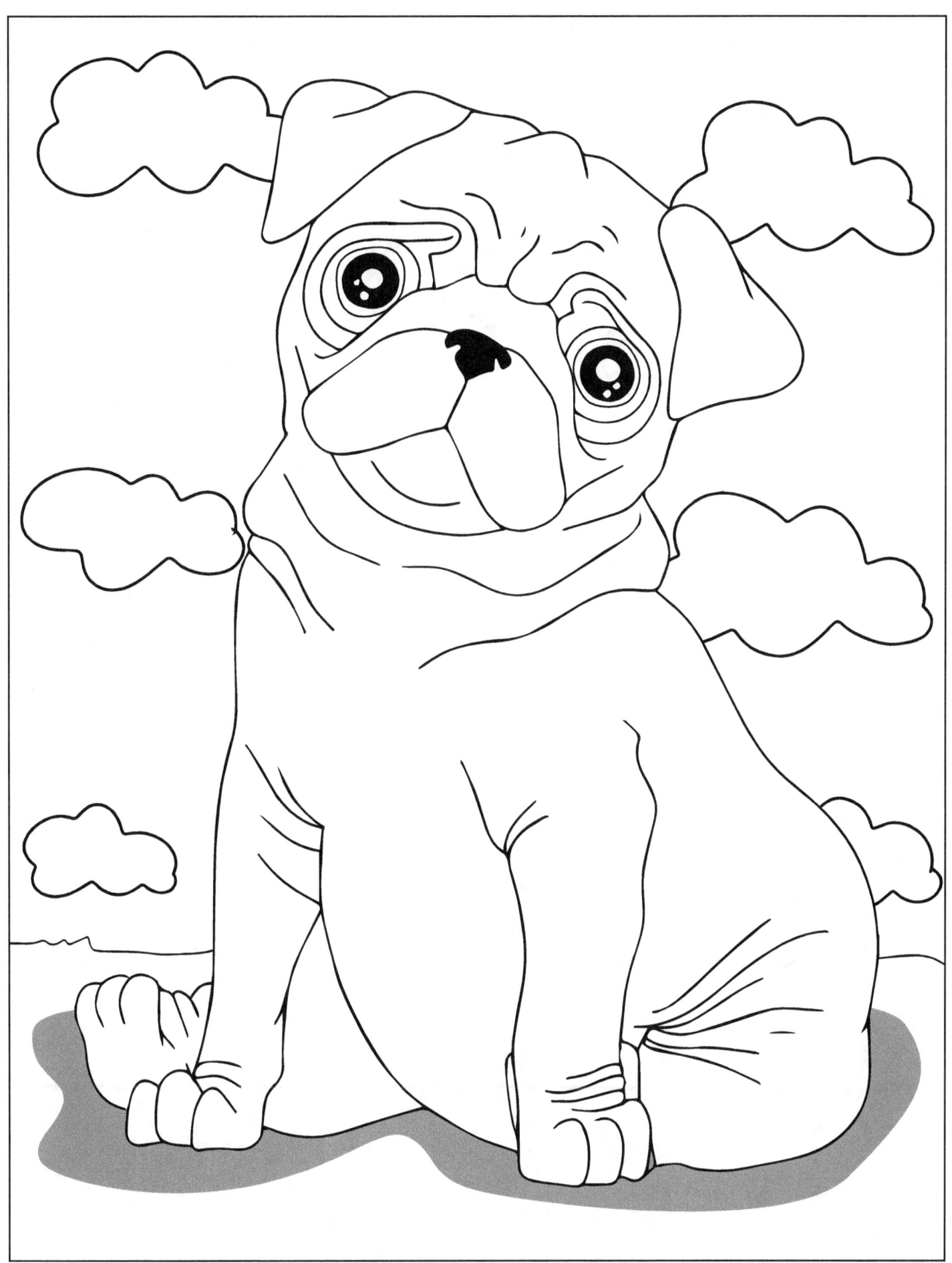

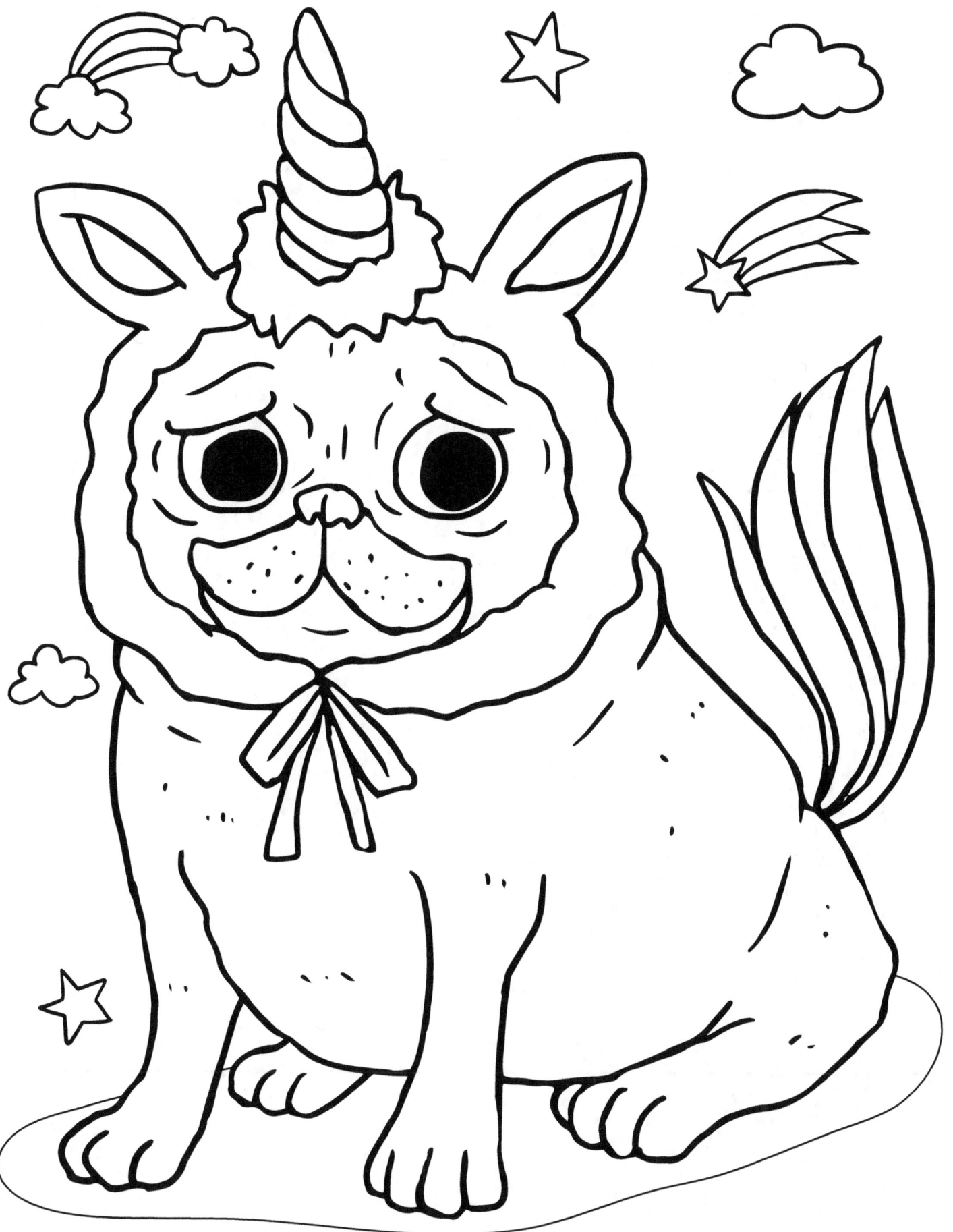

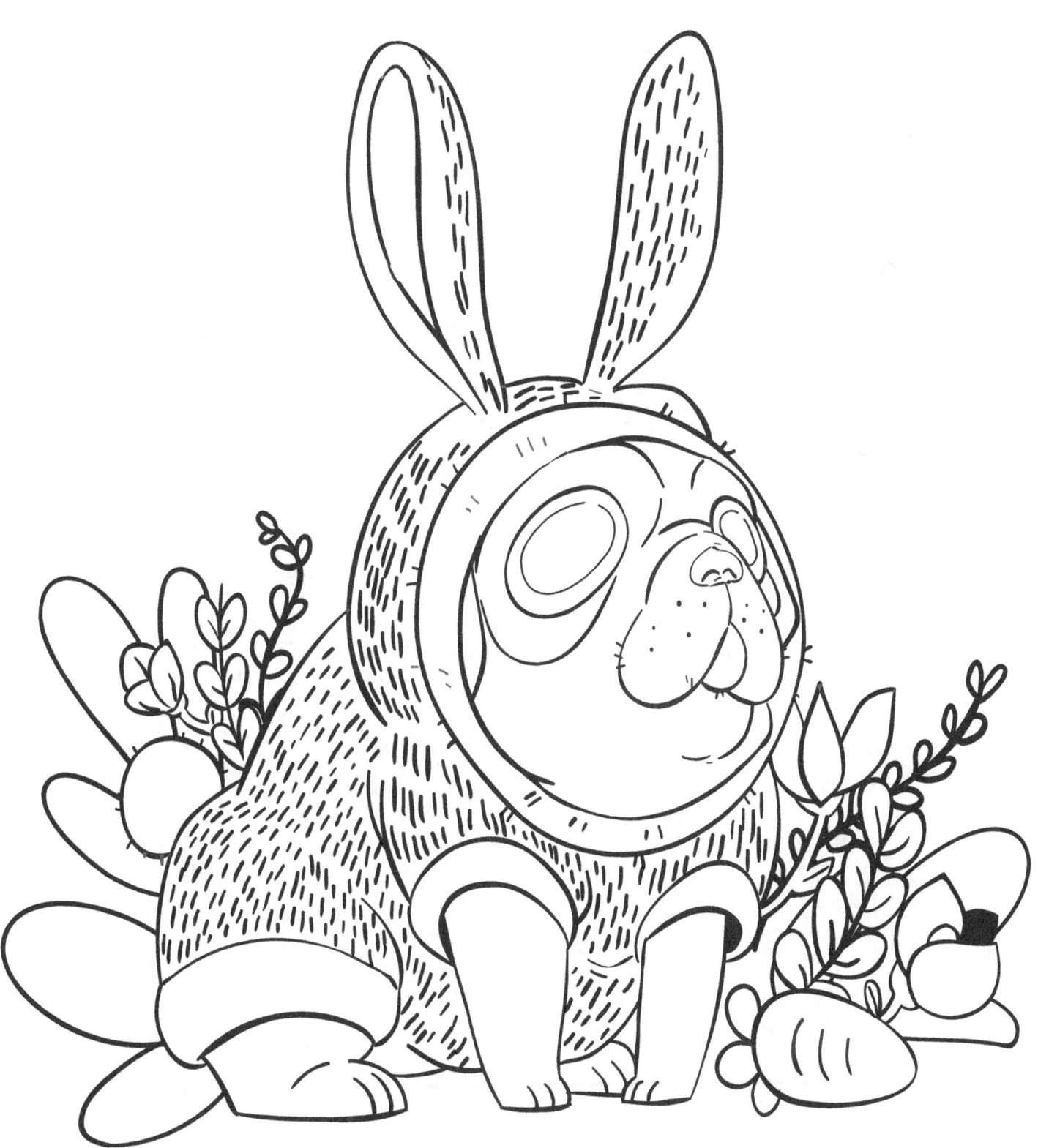

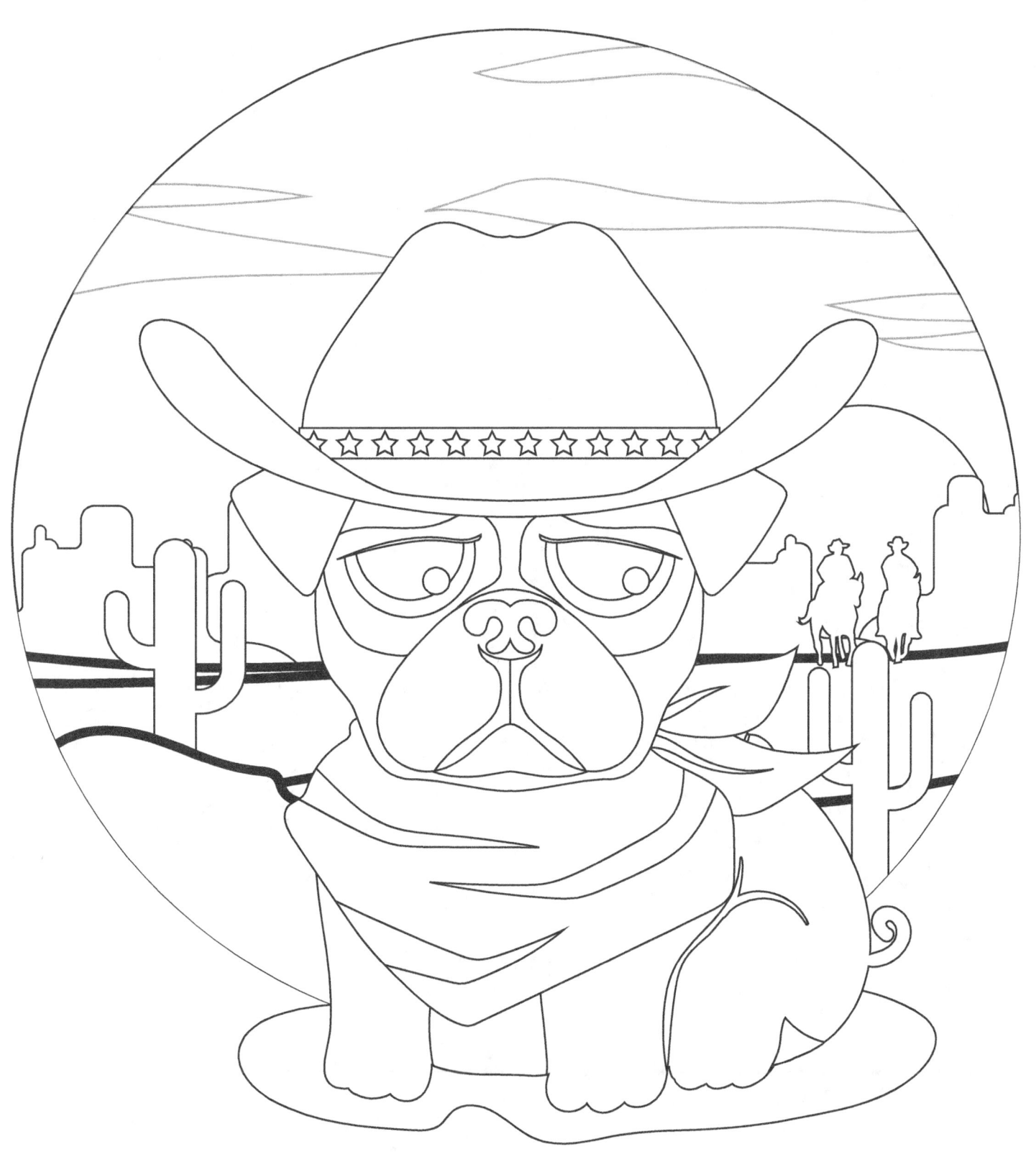

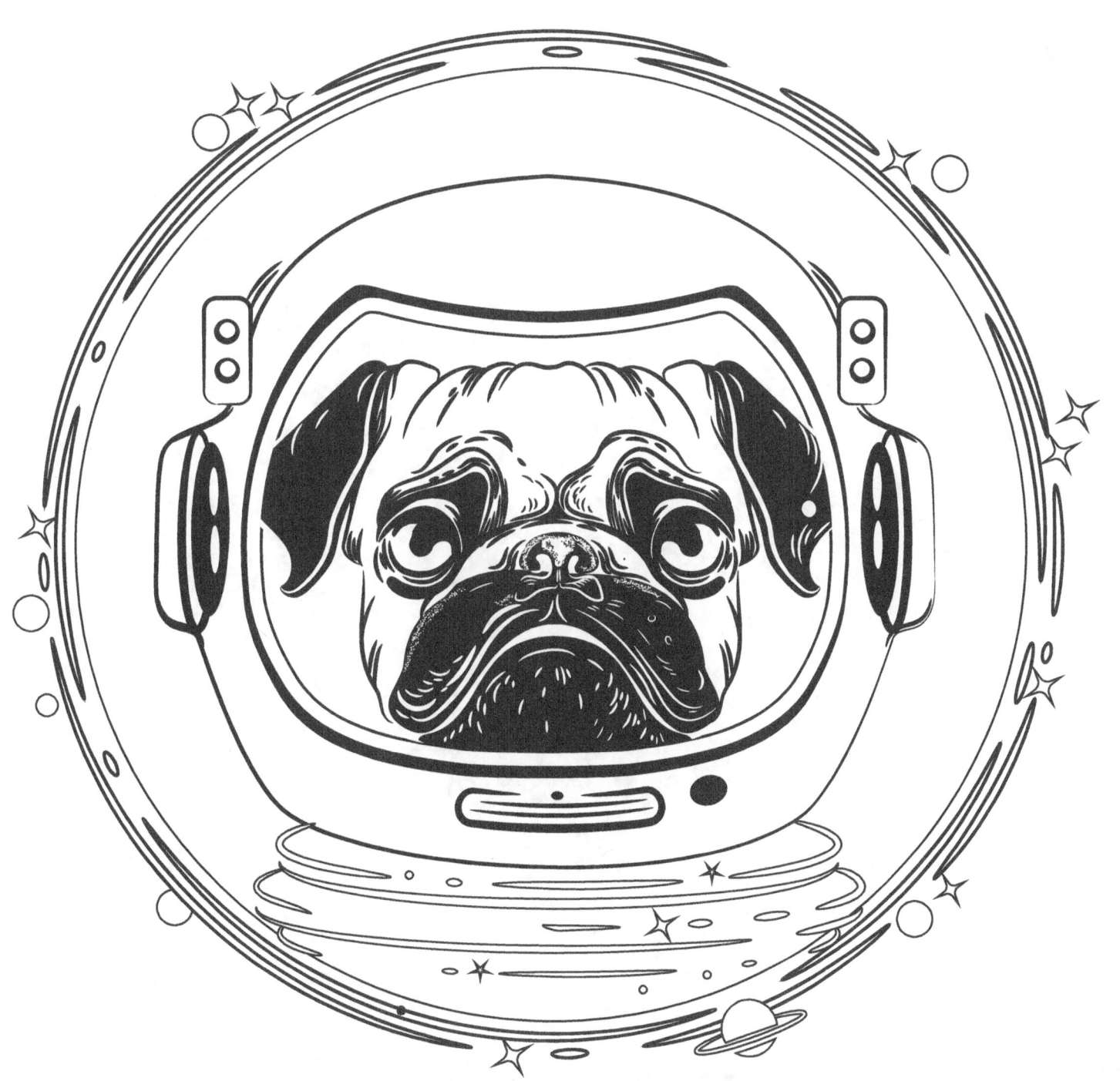

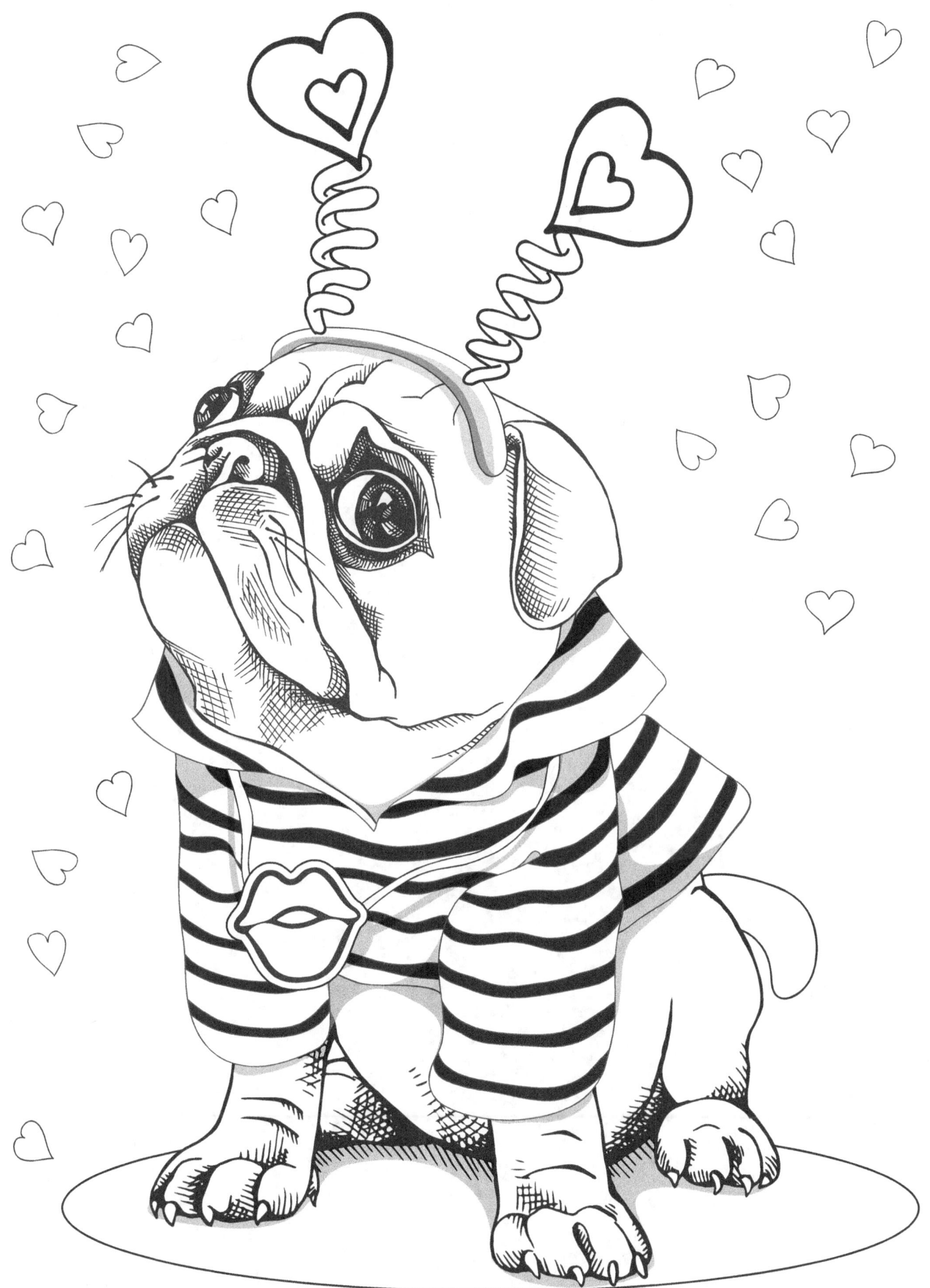

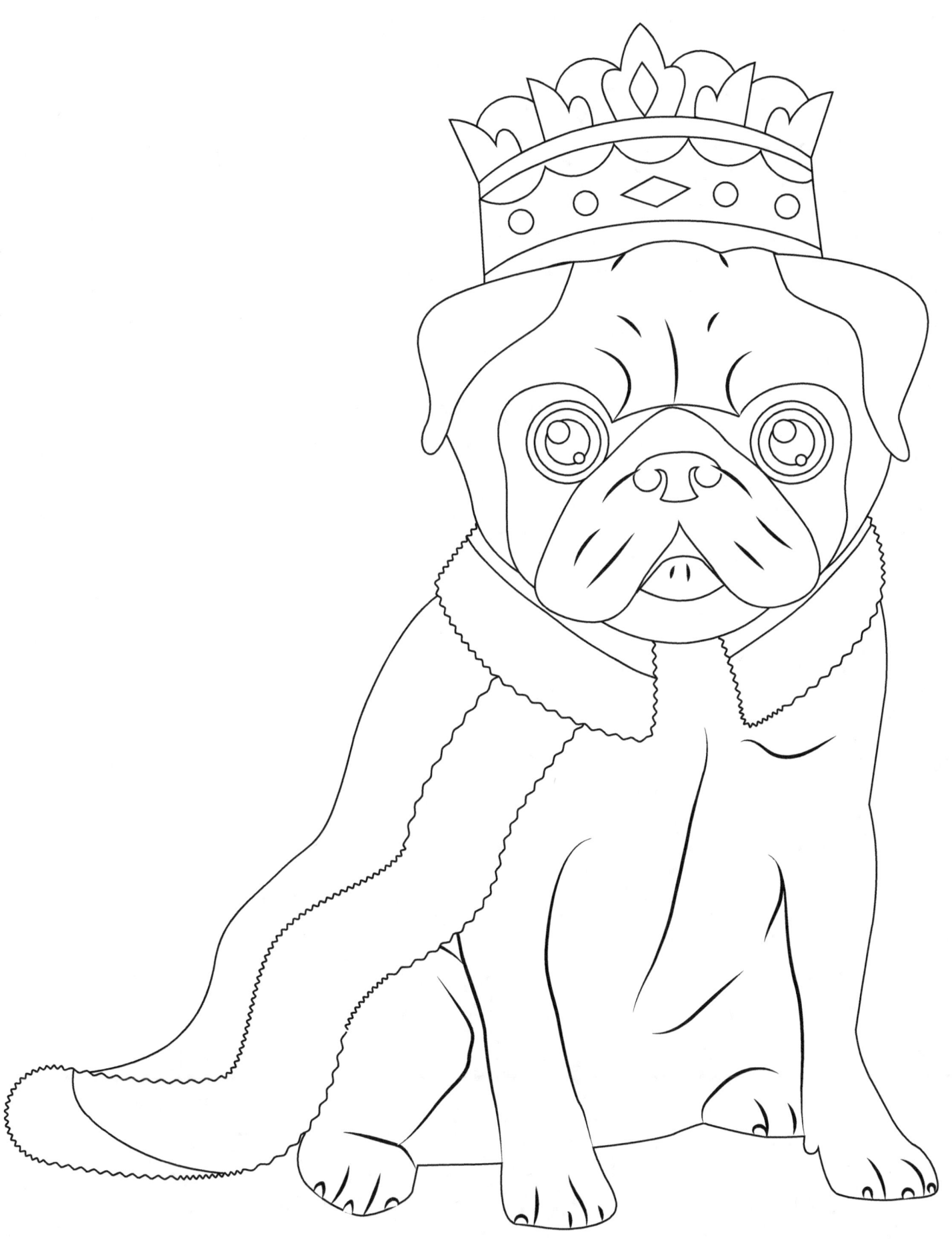

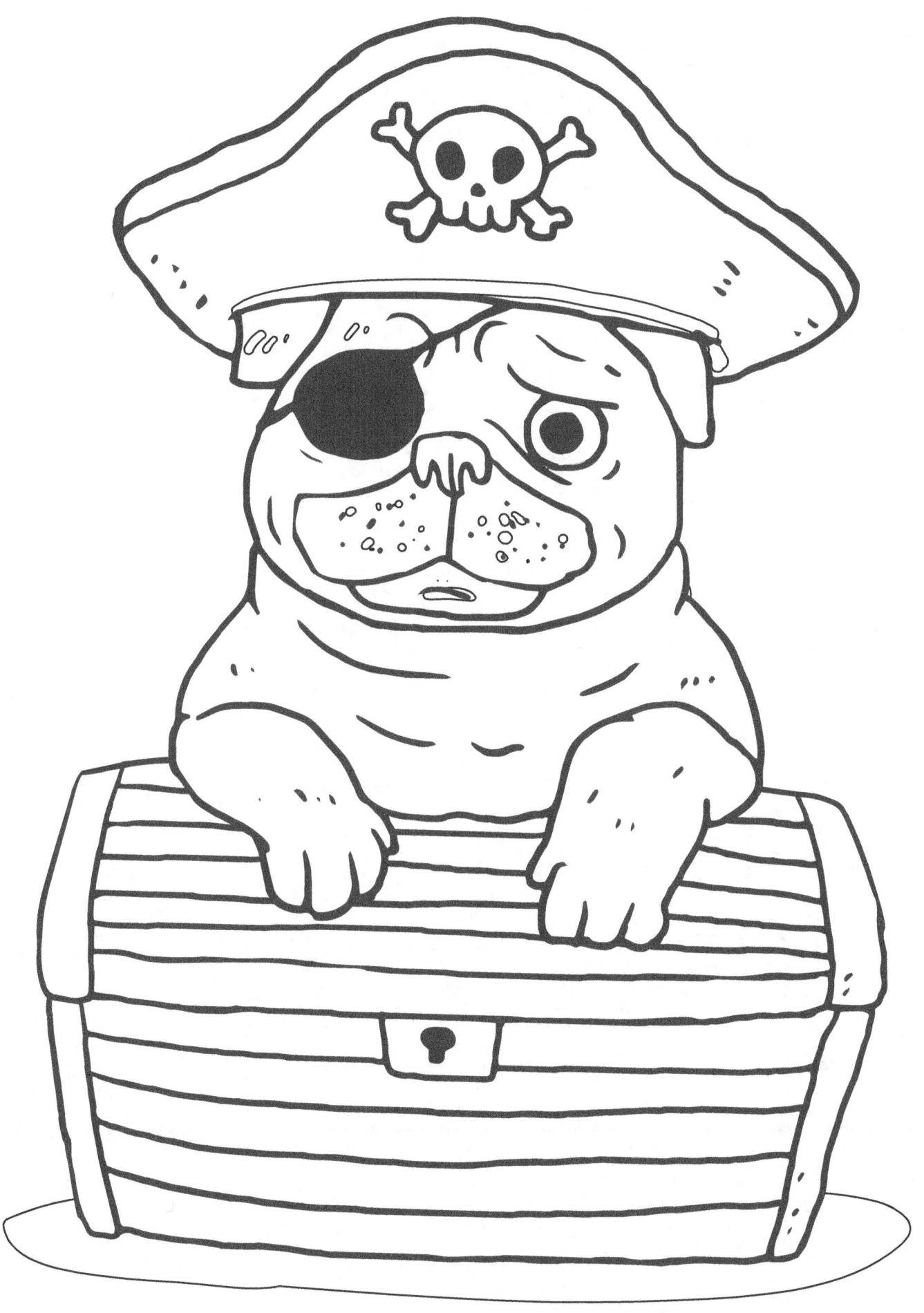

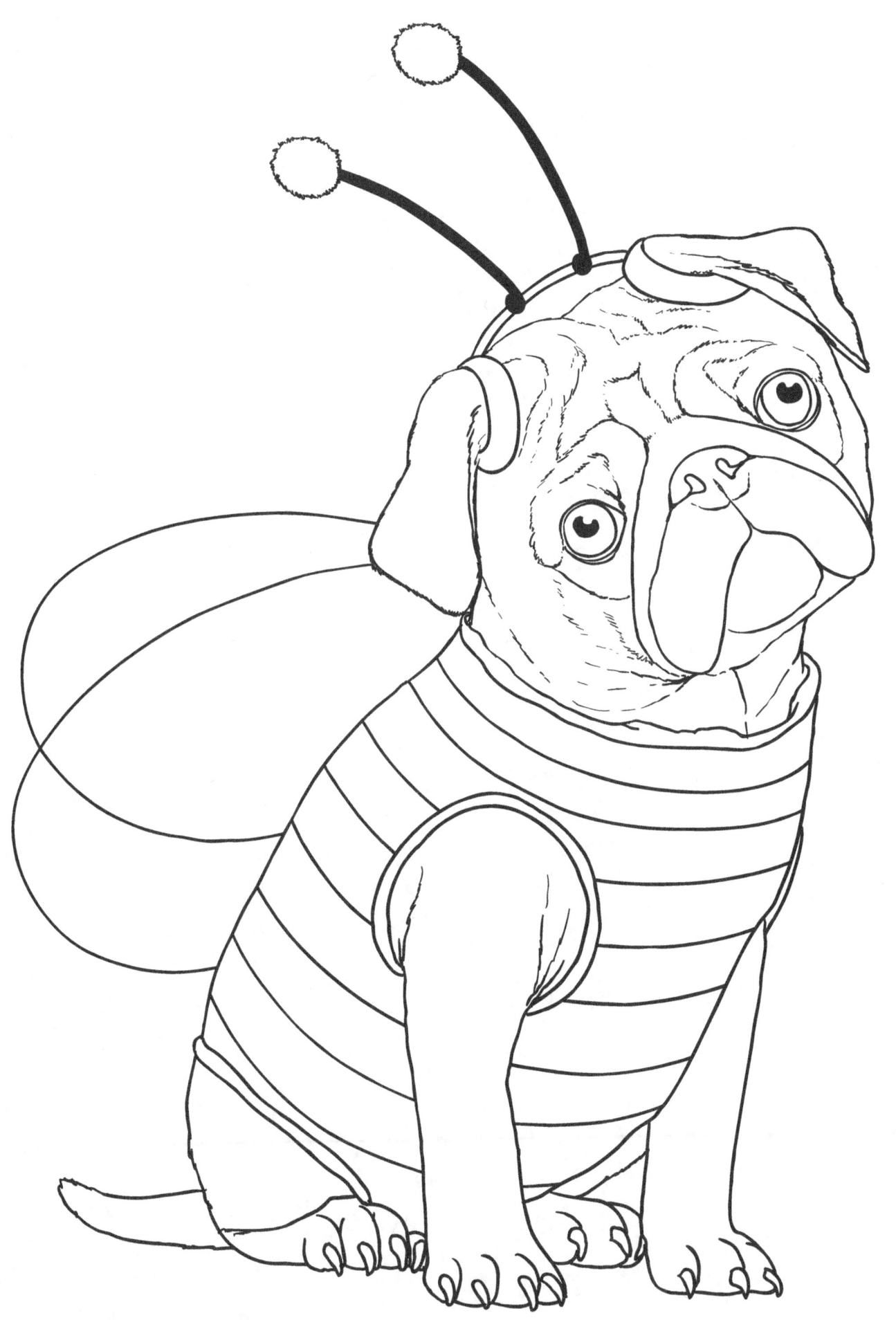

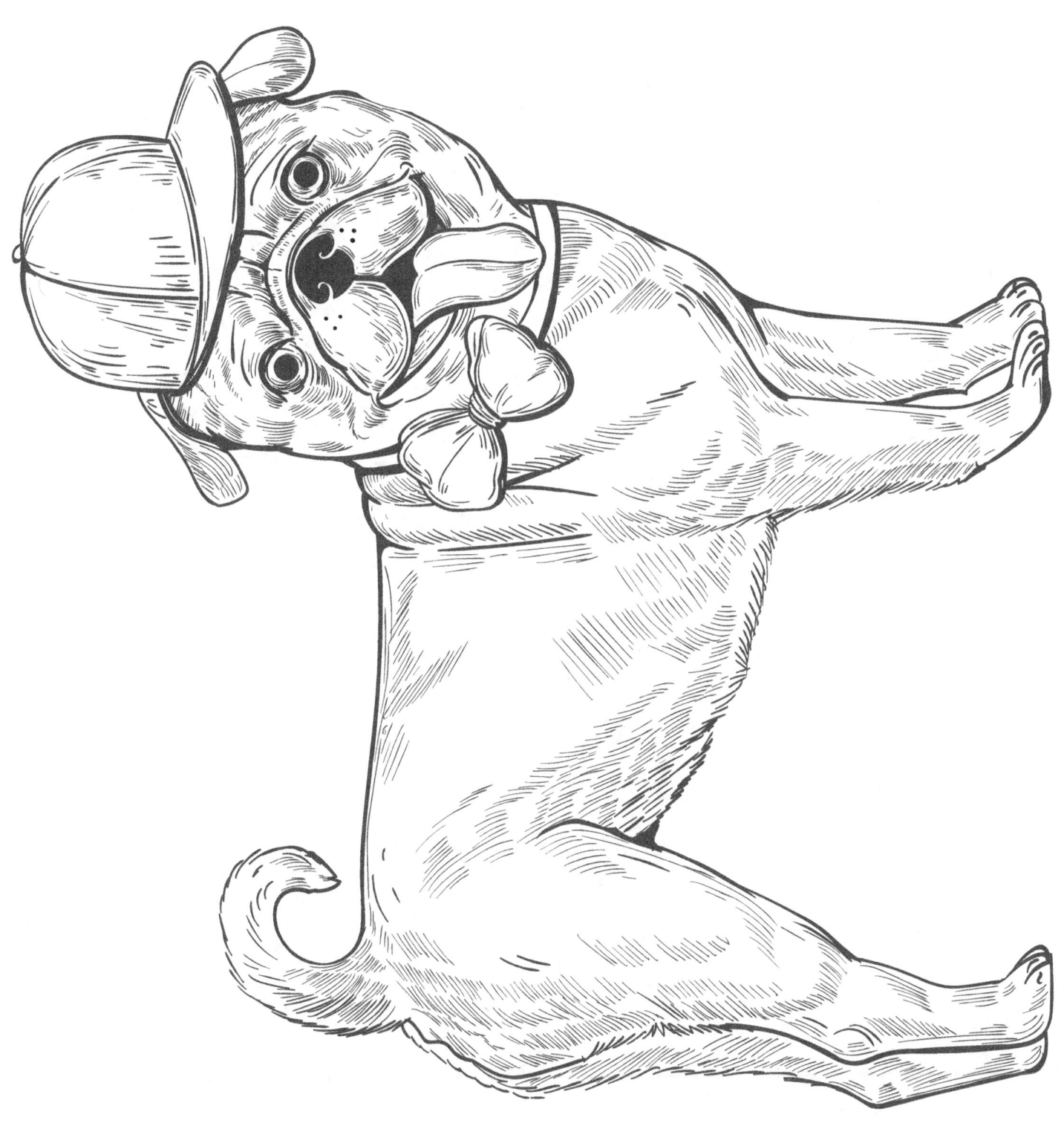

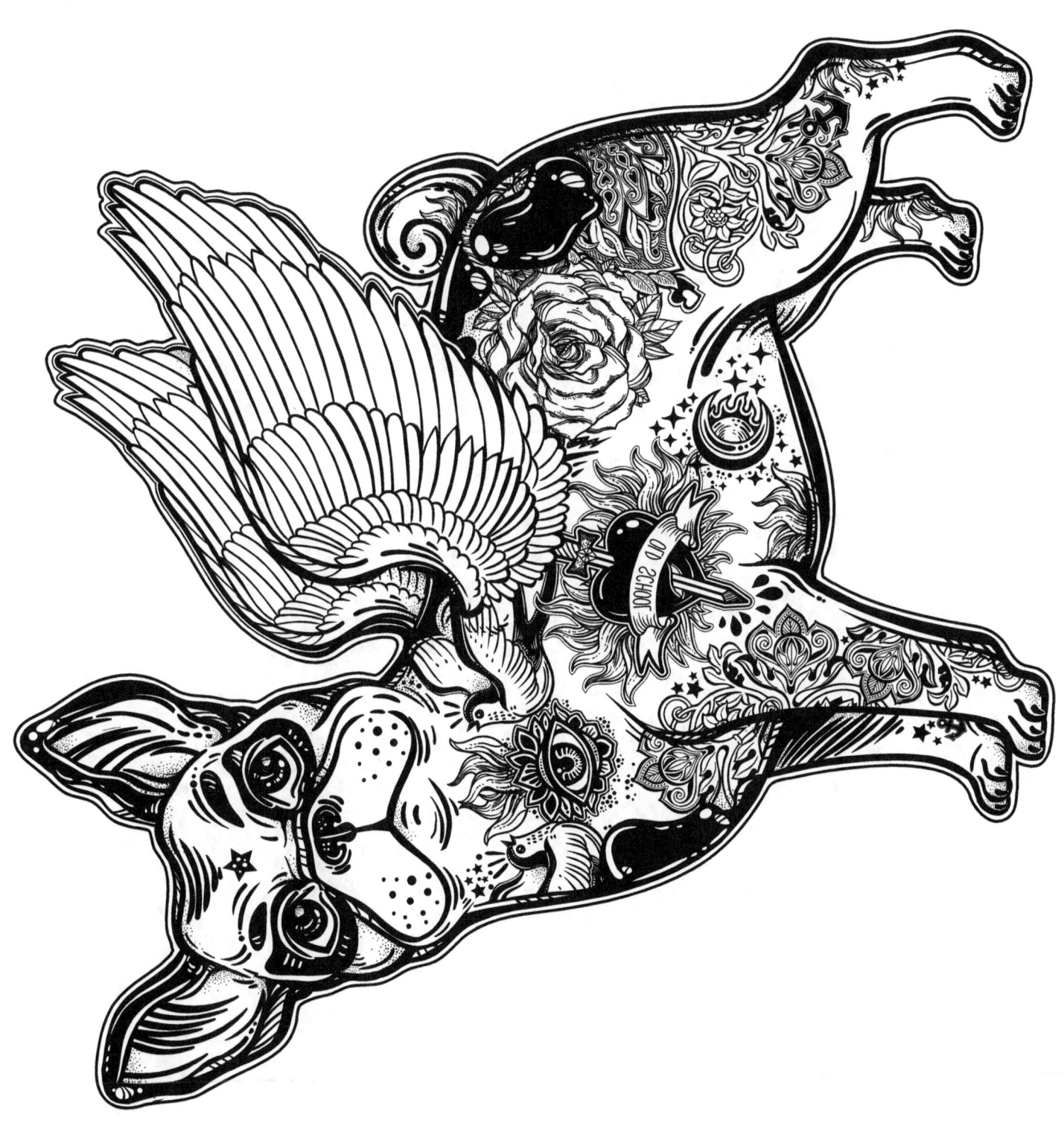

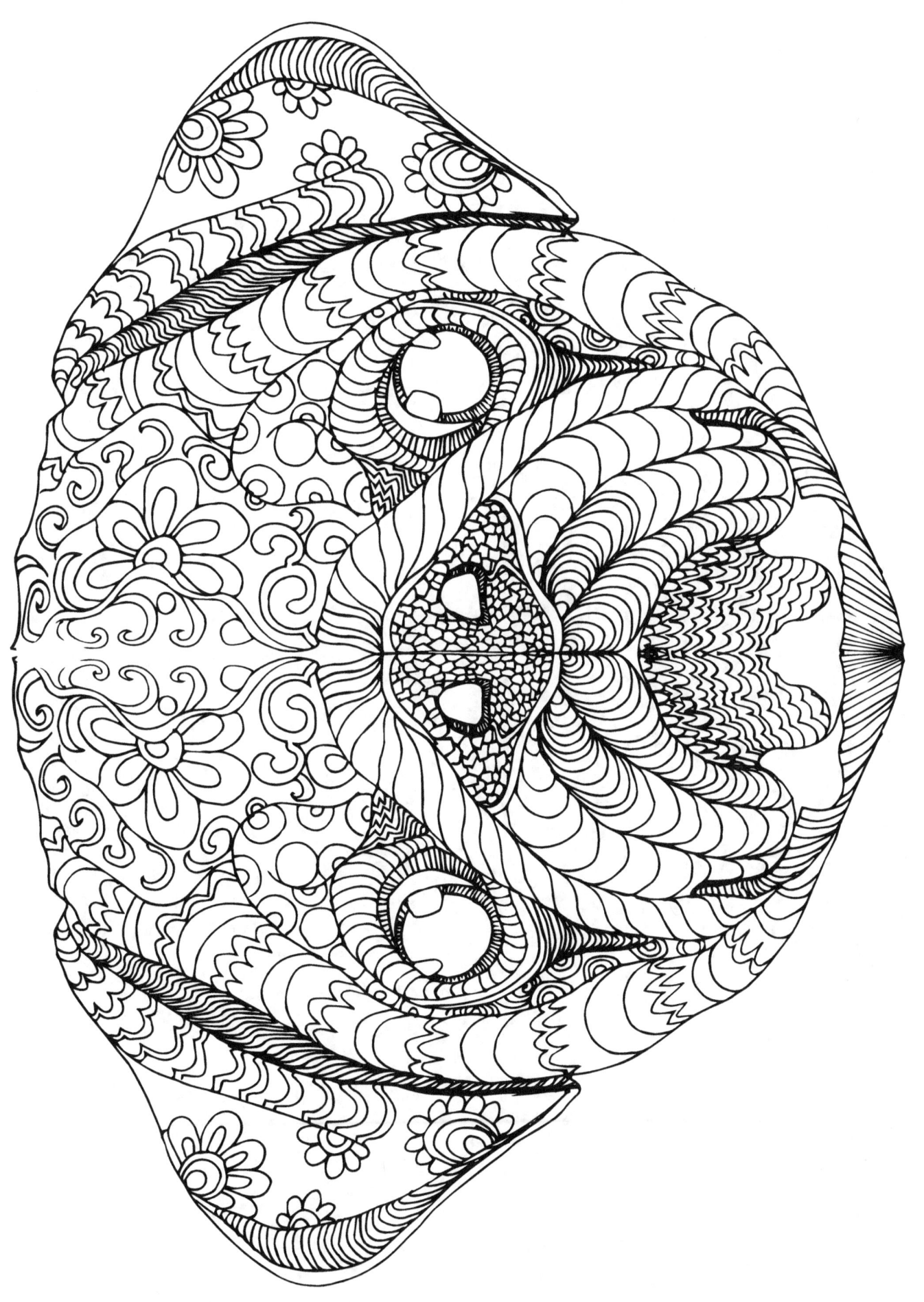

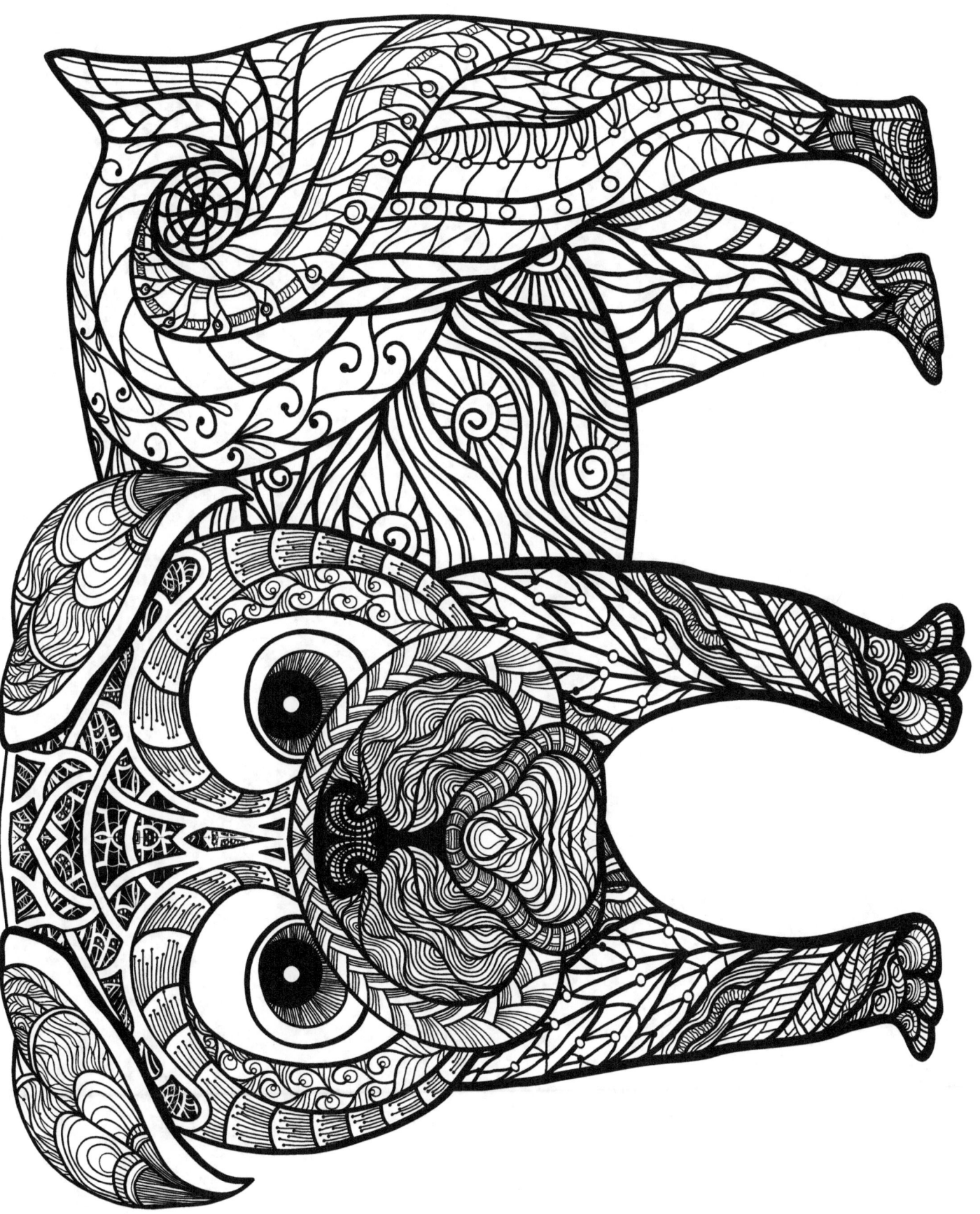

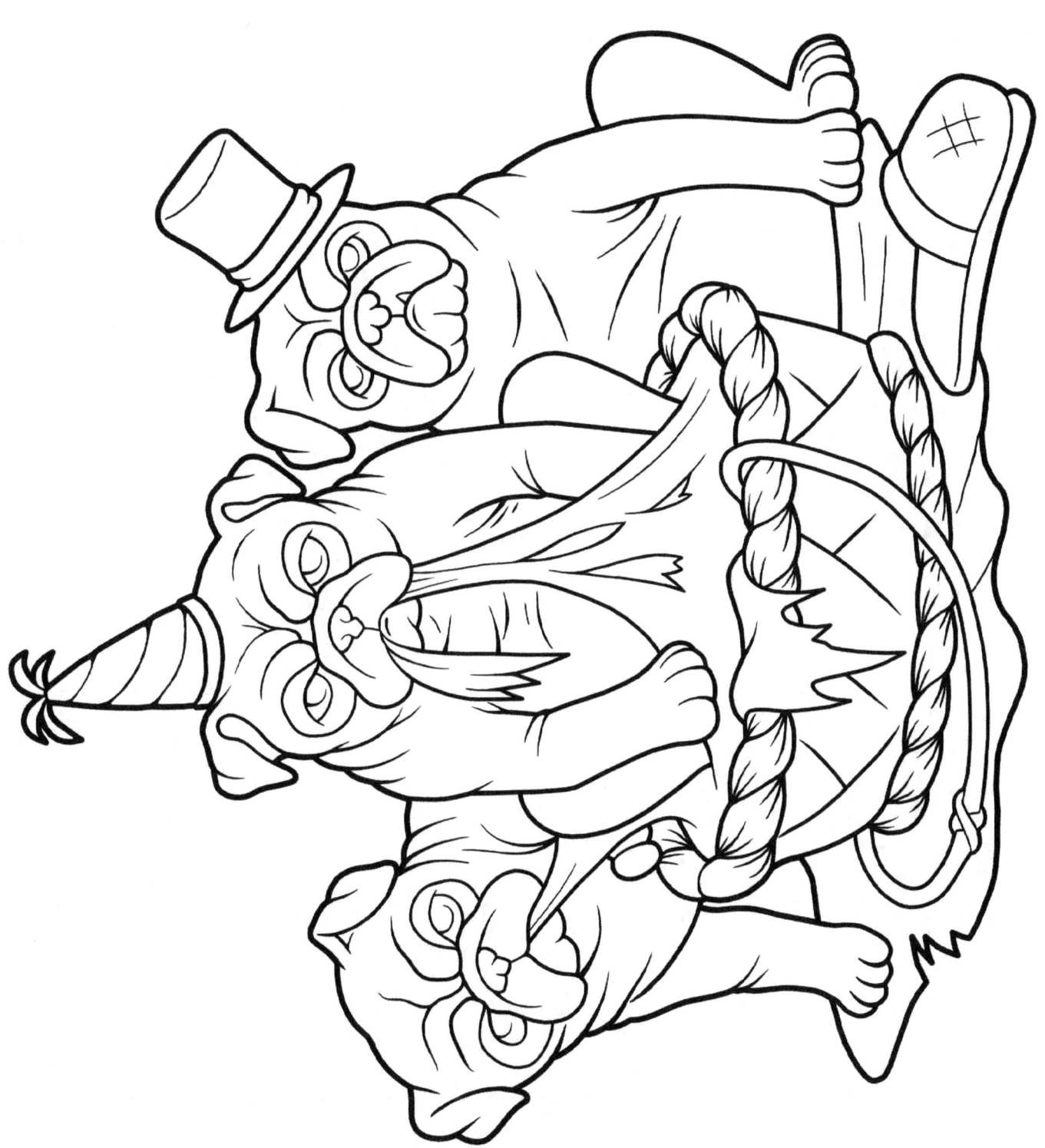

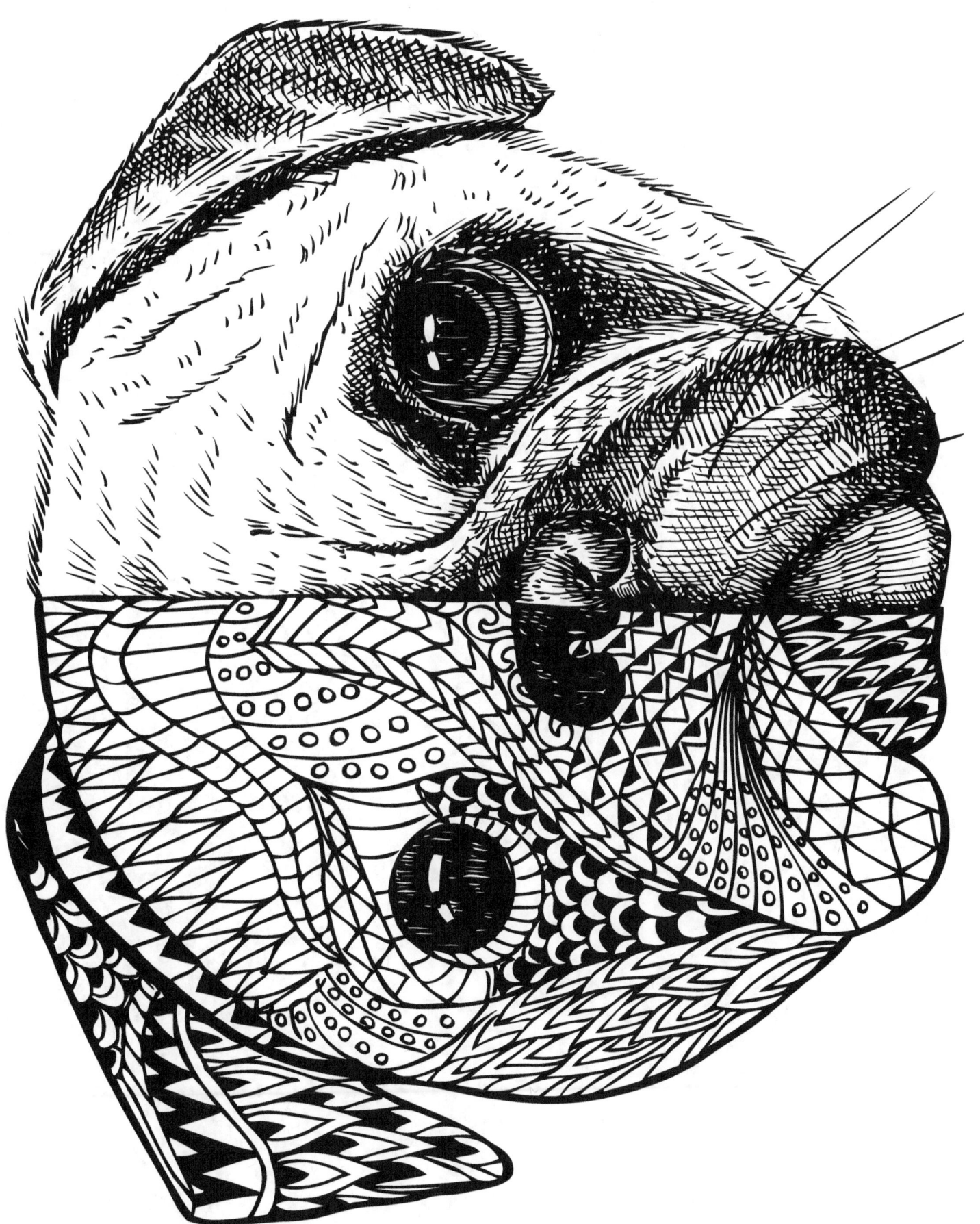

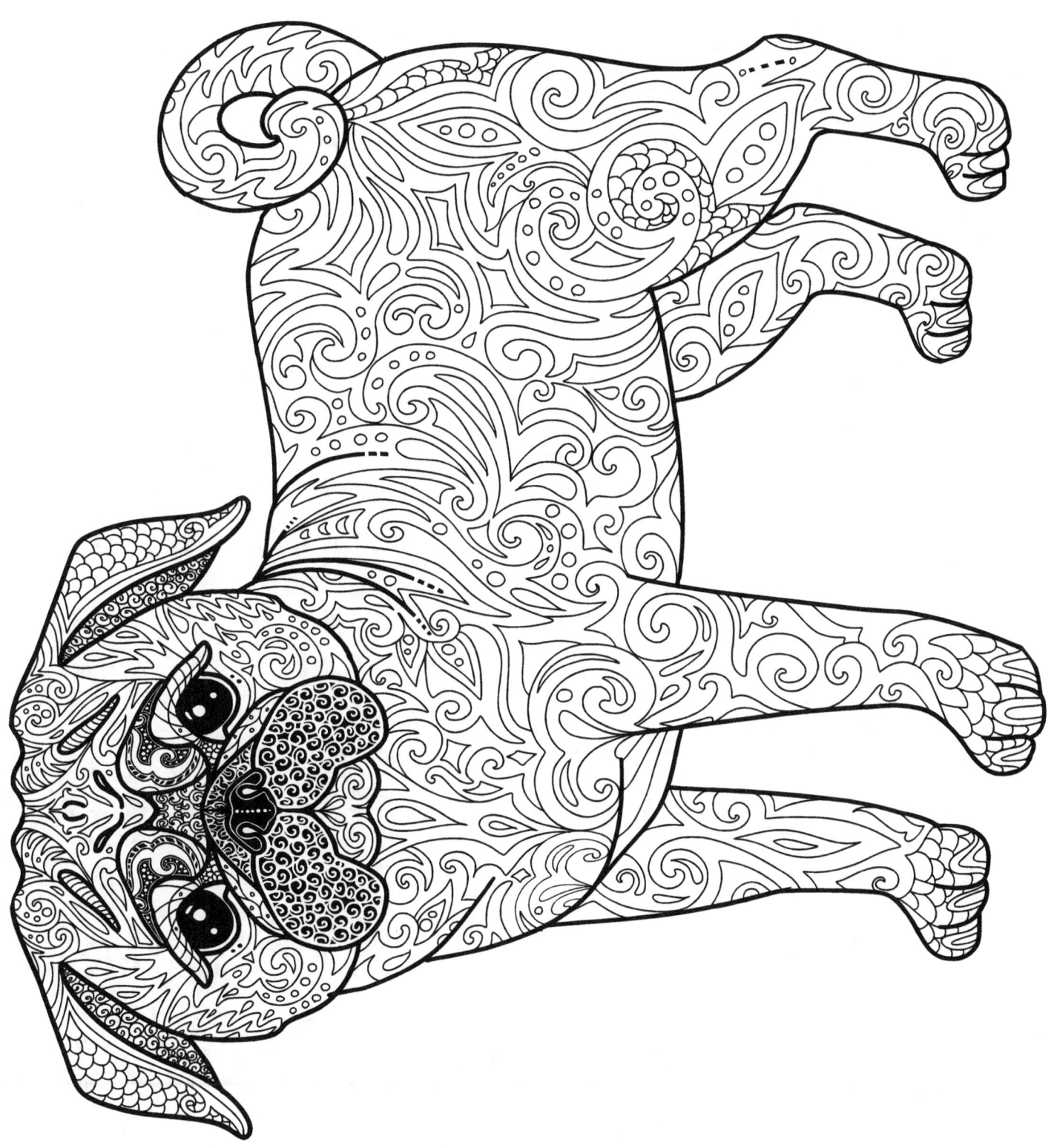

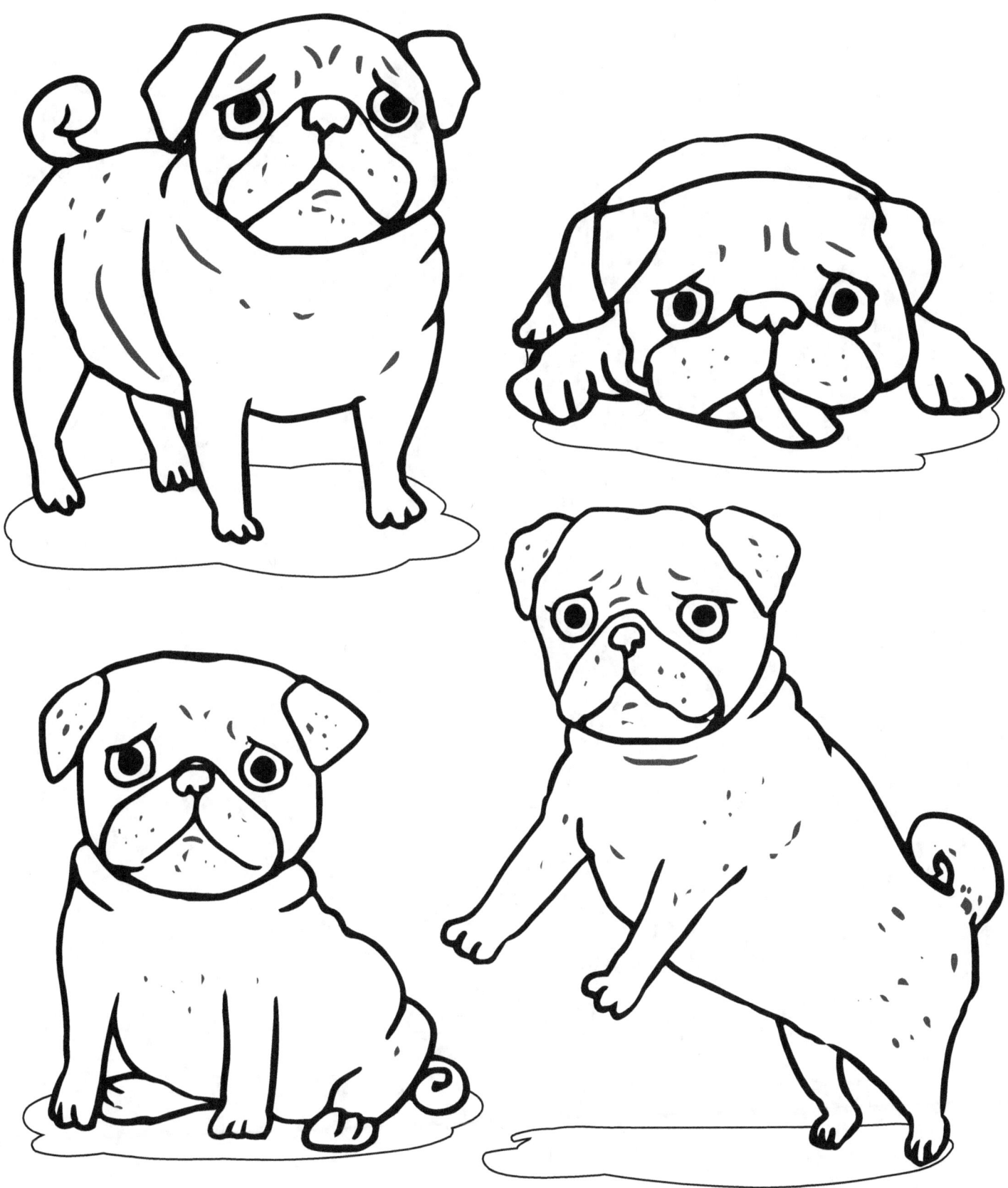

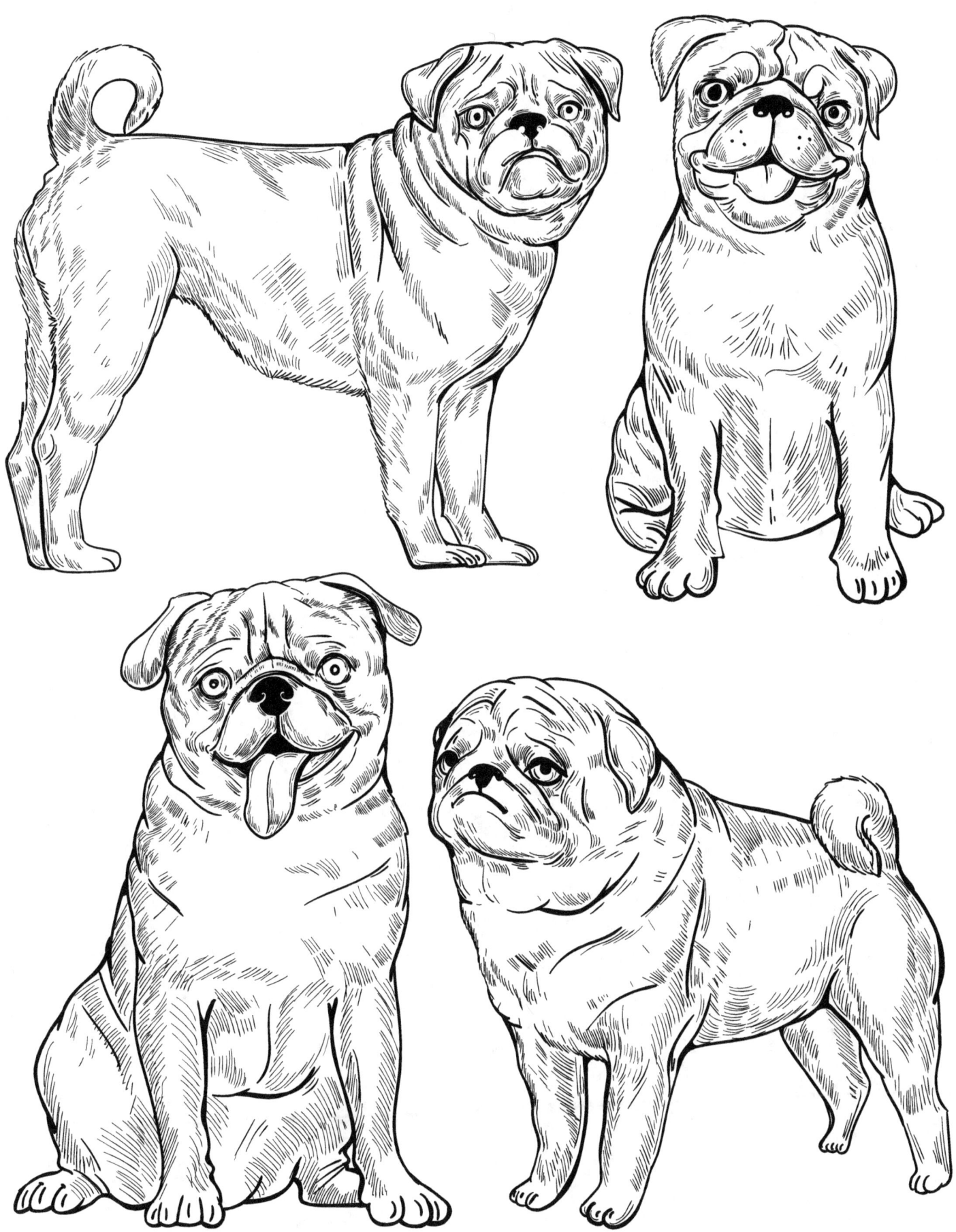

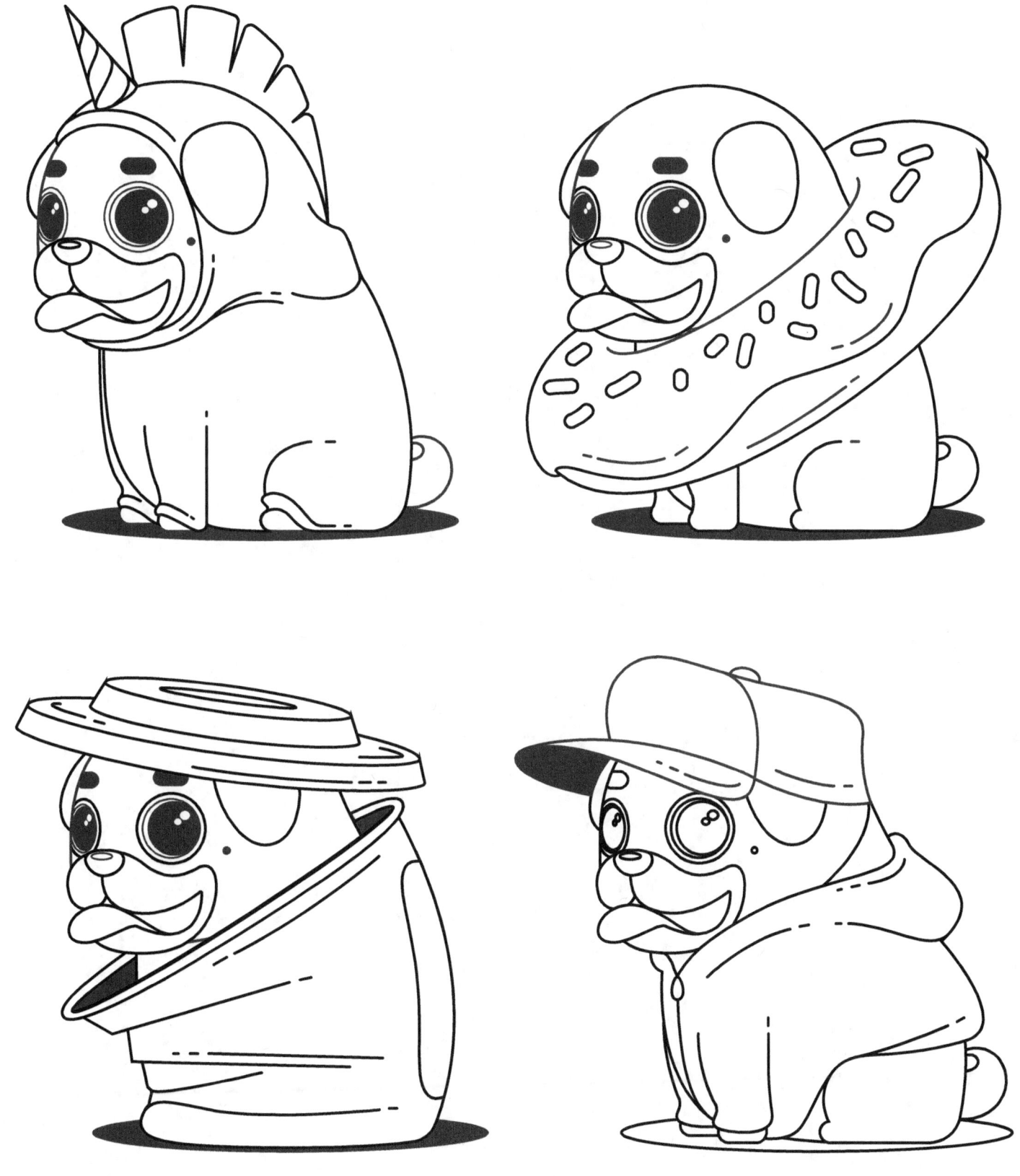

www.ingramcontent.com/pod-product-compliance
Lightning Source LLC
Chambersburg PA
CBHW062333220526
45469CB00008B/2700